P9-CBD-990

Accounting
TWENTY-SECOND EDITION

OR

Financial Accounting
TENTH EDITION

Carl S. Warren
University of Georgia, Athens

James M. Reeve
University of Tennessee, Knoxville

Jonathan E. Duchac
Wake Forest University

THOMSON

SOUTH-WESTERN

Australia · Brazil · Canada · Mexico · Singapore · Spain · United Kingdom · United States

THOMSON
SOUTH-WESTERN

Working Papers Chapters 1-17

to accompany Accounting 22e or Financial Accounting 10e

Carl S. Warren, James M. Reeve, Jonathan E. Duchac

VP/Editorial Director:
Jack W. Calhoun

Publisher:
Rob Dewey

Executive Editor:
Sharon Oblinger

Developmental Editor:
Steven E. Joos

Assistant Editor:
Erin Berger

Editorial Assistant:
Kelly Somers

Marketing Manager:
Robin Farrar

Sr. Content Project Manager:
Cliff Kallemeyn

Associate Manager of Technology:
John Barans

Sr. Technology Project Editor:
Sally Neiman

Sr. Technology Project Editor:
Robin Browning

Web Coordinator:
Karen Schaffer

Sr. First Print Buyer:
Doug Wilke

Art Director:
Bethany Casey

Photo Manager:
Tom Hill

Compositor:
Sheryl Nelson/OffCenter Concepts

Printer:
West Group
Eagan MN

EXERCISE 1-1

1. _____   6. _____   11. _____
2. _____   7. _____   12. _____
3. _____   8. _____   13. _____
4. _____   9. _____   14. _____
5. _____   10. _____   15. _____

EXERCISE 1-2

_____

_____

_____

_____

_____

_____

EXERCISE 1-3

1. _____   6. _____
2. _____   7. _____
3. _____   8. _____
4. _____   9. _____
5. _____   10. _____

EXERCISE 1-4

_____

_____

EXERCISE 1-5

_____

_____

EXERCISE 1-6

	Assets	=	Liabilities	+	Owner's Equity
a.	_____	=	$85,000	+	$215,600
b.	$93,500	=	_____	+	6,150
c.	42,500	=	11,275	+	_____

EXERCISE 1-7

a. _____

b. _____

c. _____

d. _____

e. _____

EXERCISE 1-8

a. Land: _____

b. Wages expense: _____

c. Accounts payable: _____

d. Fees earned: _____

e. Supplies: _____

f. Cash: _____

EXERCISE 1-9

a. _____

b. _____

c. _____

d. _____

e. _____

EXERCISE 1-10

a. (1) Assets: _____

   (2) Liabilities: _____

   (3) Owner's equity: _____

b. (1) Assets: _____

   (2) Liabilities: _____

   (3) Owner's equity: _____

EXERCISE 1-11

1. Revenues: _____

2. Expenses: _____

3. Owner's investments: _____

4. Owner's withdrawals: _____

EXERCISE 1-12

1. _____   6. _____

2. _____   7. _____

3. _____   8. _____

4. _____   9. _____

5. _____   10. _____

EXERCISE 1-13

a. (1) _____

   (2) _____

   (3) _____

   (4) _____

   (5) _____

   (6) _____

   (7) _____

b. _____

c. _____

d. _____

e. _____

EXERCISE 1-14

_____

_____

_____

EXERCISE 1-15

Alpha:

Bravo:

Charlie:

Delta:

EXERCISE 1-16

1. Accounts Payable: _____

2. Cash: _____

3. Fees Earned: _____

4. Ishmael Maya, Capital: _____

5. Land: _____

6. Supplies: _____

7. Supplies Expense: _____

8. Utilities Expense: _____

9. Wages Expense: _____

10. Wages Payable: _____

EXERCISE 1-17

1. Accounts Payable: _____

2. Cash: _____

3. Fees Earned: _____

4. Ishmael Maya, Capital: _____

5. Land: _____

6. Supplies: _____

7. Supplies Expense: _____

8. Utilities Expense: _____

9. Wages Expense: _____

10. Wages Payable: _____

EXERCISE 1-18

Statement of Owner's Equity

EXERCISE 1-19

	Income Statement								

EXERCISE 1-20

Oscar						
Papa:						
Quebec:						
Romeo						

EXERCISE 1-21

a.

EXERCISE 1-22

  a. Accounts payable: _____

  b. Cash equivalents: _____

  c. Crude oil inventory: _____

  d. Equipment: _____

  e. Exploration expenses: _____

  f. Income taxes payable: _____

  g. Investments: _____

  h. Long-term debt: _____

  i. Marketable securities: _____

  j. Notes and loans payable: _____

  k. Notes receivable: _____

  l. Operating expenses: _____

  m. Prepaid taxes: _____

  n. Sales: _____

  o. Selling expenses: _____

EXERCISE 1-23

  1. Cash received as owner's investment: _____

  2. Cash received from fees earned: _____

  3. Cash paid for land: _____

  4. Cash paid for expenses: _____

EXERCISE 1-24

Statement of Cash Flows

EXERCISE 1-25

EXERCISE 1-25 (optional) Continued

Income Statement

Statement of Owner's Equity

EXERCISE 1-25 (optional) Concluded

Balance Sheet

This Page Not Used.

PROBLEM 1-3 ___

1. *Omit "00" in the cents columns.*

	Income Statement					

2. *Omit "00" in the cents columns.*

	Statement of Owner's Equity					

PROBLEM 1-3 ___ , Concluded

3. *Omit "00" in the cents columns.*

Balance Sheet

4. *Omit "00" in the cents columns.*

Statement of Cash Flows

PROBLEM 1-4 _____

1.

	ASSETS		=	LIABILITIES	+	OWNER'S EQUITY							
	Cash	+ Supplies	=	Accounts Payable	+	Capital	− Drawing	+ Sales Comm.	− Office Sal. Exp.	− Rent Exp.	− Auto Exp.	− Supp. Exp.	− Misc. Exp.
a.													
bal.													
b.													
bal.													
c.													
bal.													
d.													
bal.													
e.													
bal.													
f.													
bal.													
g.													
bal.													
h.													
bal.													
i.													
bal.													

PROBLEM 1-4 ___, Continued

2. *Omit "00" in the cents columns.*

Income Statement

Statement of Owner's Equity

PROBLEM 1-4 ___, Concluded

Balance Sheet

This Page Not Used.

PROBLEM 1-5 ___

1.

		ASSETS				=	LIABILITIES	+	OWNER'S EQUITY
Cash	+	Accounts Receivable	+	Supplies	+	Land	=	Accounts Payable	+	Capital

, Capital

, Capital

, Capital

Name _____

Chapter 1

PROBLEM 1-5____, Continued

2.

	ASSETS			=	LIABILITIES +			OWNER'S EQUITY							
Cash +	Accts. Rec. +	Supplies +	Land =		Accts. Pay.	+ Capital –	Drawing +	Dry Cleaning Sales	– Dry Cleaning Exp. –	Wages Exp. –	. Rent Exp. –	Supplies Exp. –	Truck Exp. –	Util. Exp. –	Misc. Exp.
a.															
b.															
c.															
d.															
e.															
f.															
g.															
h.															
i.															
j.															
k.															
l.															

PROBLEM 1-5 ___ , Continued

Omit "00" in the cents columns.

Income Statement

3b. *Omit "00" in the cents columns.*

Statement of Owner's Equity

PROBLEM 1-5 ___ , Continued

3c. *Omit "00" in the cents columns.*

Balance Sheet

PROBLEM 1-5 ___ , Concluded

4. *Omit "00" in the cents columns.*

	Statement of Cash Flows				

This Page Not Used.

PROBLEM 1-6 ___

a. _____

b. _____

c. _____

d. _____

e. _____

f. _____

g. _____

h. _____

i. _____

j. _____

k. _____

l. _____

m. _____

n. _____

o. _____

p. _____

q. _____

32

This Page Not Used.

CONTINUING PROBLEM

1.

	ASSETS			=	LIABILITIES +		OWNER'S EQUITY						
	Cash +	Accts. Rec. +	Supplies =		Accts. Pay. +	Kris Payne, Capital −	Kris Payne, Drawing +	Fees Earned −	Music Exp. −	Office Rent Exp. −	Equip. Rent Exp. −	Adv. Exp. −	Wage Exp. −	Util. Exp. −	Sup. Exp. −	Misc. Exp.
4/1														
4/2														
bal.														
4/4														
bal.														
4/6														
bal.														
4/8														
bal.														
4/12														
bal.														
4/13														
bal.														
4/16														
bal.														
4/22														
bal.														
4/25														
bal.														
4/29														
bal.														
4/30														
bal.														
4/30														
bal.														

Chapter 1

CONTINUING PROBLEM (Continued)

1.

	ASSETS		= LIABILITIES +	OWNER'S EQUITY										
	Cash +	Accts. Rec. +	Supplies =	Accts. Pay.	+ Kris Payne, Capital −	Kris Payne, Drawing +	Fees Earned −	Music Exp. −	Office Rent Exp. −	Equip. Rent Exp. −	Adv. Exp. −	Wage Exp. −	Util. Exp. −	Sup. Exp. −	Misc. Exp.
bal.														
4/30														
bal.														
4/30														
bal.														
4/30														
bal.														
4/30														
bal.														

34

CONTINUING PROBLEM, Continued

2. *Omit "00" in the cents columns.*

Income Statement

3. *Omit "00" in the cents columns.*

Statement of Owner's Equity

CONTINUING PROBLEM, Concluded

4. *Omit "00" in the cents columns.*

Balance Sheet

EXERCISE 2-1

Accounts Payable: _____

Air Traffic Liability: _____

Aircraft Fuel Expense: _____

Cargo and Mail Revenue: _____

Commissions: _____

Flight Equipment: _____

Landing Fees: _____

Passenger Revenue: _____

Purchase Deposits for Flight Equipment: _____

Spare Parts and Supplies: _____

EXERCISE 2-2

Account	Account Number
Accounts Payable..................	_____
Accounts Receivable.............	_____
Angie Stowe, Capital.............	_____
Angie Stowe, Drawing...........	_____
Cash......................................	_____
Fees Earned.........................	_____
Land......................................	_____
Miscellaneous Expense	_____
Supplies Expense.................	_____
Wages Expense	_____

EXERCISE 2-3

Balance Sheet Accounts		**Income Statement Accounts**	
Acct #	Account Name	Acct #	Account Name
	1. Assets		4. Revenue
			5. Expenses
	2. Liabilities		
	3. Owner's Equity		

EXERCISE 2-4

a. and b.

Transaction	Account Debited — Type	Effect	Account Credited — Type	Effect
(1)	asset	+	owner's equity	+
(2)				
(3)				
(4)				
(5)				
(6)				
(7)				
(8)				
(9)				

EXERCISE 2-5

JOURNAL   PAGE

	DATE	DESCRIPTION	POST. REF.	DEBIT	CREDIT	
1						1
2						2
3						3
4						4
5						5
6						6
7						7
8						8
9						9
10						10
11						11
12						12
13						13
14						14
15						15
16						16
17						17
18						18
19						19
20						20
21						21

EXERCISE 2-5, Concluded

JOURNAL

	DATE		DESCRIPTION	POST. REF.	DEBIT	CREDIT	
1							1
2							2
3							3
4							4
5							5
6							6
7							7
8							

EXERCISE 2-6

Unadjusted Trial Balance

EXERCISE 2-7

1. Accounts Payable: _____

2. Accounts Receivable: _____

3. Cash: _____

4. Fees Earned: _____

5. Insurance Expense: _____

6. Keith Dupree, Drawing: _____

7. Supplies Expense: _____

EXERCISE 2-8

a. Accounts Payable: _____

b. Accounts Receivable: _____

d. Boyd Magnus, Capital: _____

e. Boyd Magnus, Drawing: _____

c. Cash: _____

f. Fees Earned: _____

g. Office Equipment: _____

h. Rent Expense: _____

i. Supplies: _____

j. Wages Expense: _____

EXERCISE 2-9

	Increase	Decrease	Normal Balance
Balance sheet accounts:			
Asset....................................	**(a)** _____	Credit	**(b)** _____
Liability..................................	**(c)** _____	**(d)** _____	Credit
Owner's Equity:			
Capital	Credit	**(e)** _____	**(f)** _____
Drawing	**(g)** _____	**(h)** _____	Debit
Income statement accounts:			
Revenue	**(i)** _____	**(j)** _____	**(k)** _____
Expense.............................	Debit	**(l)** _____	Debit

EXERCISE 2-10

a. _____

_____

b. _____

_____

_____

EXERCISE 2-11

a. _____

_____

_____

b. _____

EXERCISE 2-12

a. _____

b. _____

c. _____

EXERCISE 2-13

JOURNAL

PAGE

	DATE		DESCRIPTION	POST. REF.	DEBIT	CREDIT	
1							1
2							2
3							3
4							4
5							5
6							6
7							7
8							8
9							9
10							10
11							11
12							12
13							13
14							14
15							15
16							16
17							17
18							18
19							19
20							
21							
22							
23							
24							
25							
26							
27							
28							
29							
30							
31							
32							

EXERCISE 2-14

a.

		JOURNAL				PAGE 38

	DATE	DESCRIPTION	POST. REF.	DEBIT	CREDIT	
1						1
2						2
3						3
4						4

b., c., d.

ACCOUNT _____ ACCOUNT NO. _____

DATE	ITEM	POST. REF.	DEBIT	CREDIT	BALANCE DEBIT	BALANCE CREDIT

ACCOUNT _____ ACCOUNT NO. _____

DATE	ITEM	POST. REF.	DEBIT	CREDIT	BALANCE DEBIT	BALANCE CREDIT

EXERCISE 2-15

a.

		JOURNAL				PAGE

	DATE	DESCRIPTION	POST. REF.	DEBIT	CREDIT	
1						1
2						2
3						3
4						4
5						5
6						6
7						7
8						8
9						9
10						10
11						11

EXERCISE 2-15, Concluded

b.

Cash	Accounts Payable

Supplies	Fees Earned

Accounts Receivable

EXERCISE 2-16

Unadjusted Trial Balance

EXERCISE 2-17

_____
_____
_____
_____
_____

EXERCISE 2-18

Unadjusted Trial Balance

EXERCISE 2-19

Error	(a) Out of Balance	(b) Difference	(c) Larger Total
1.	yes	$5,125	debit
2.			
3.			
4.			
5.			
6.			
7.			

EXERCISE 2-20

_____

_____

_____

_____

_____

_____

_____

_____

_____

Unadjusted Trial Balance (optional)

EXERCISE 2-21

JOURNAL

PAGE _____

	DATE		DESCRIPTION	POST. REF.	DEBIT	CREDIT	
1							1
2							2
3							3
4							4
5							5

EXERCISE 2-22

JOURNAL

PAGE _____

	DATE		DESCRIPTION	POST. REF.	DEBIT	CREDIT	
1							1
2							2
3							3
4							4
5							5
6							6
7							7
8							8
9							9

This Page Not Used.

PROBLEM 2-1 ___

1. and 2.

Cash

Accounts Receivable

Supplies

Prepaid Insurance

Automobiles

PROBLEM 2-1 ___ , Continued

Equipment

Notes Payable

Accounts Payable

_____ , *Capital*

Professional Fees

Rent Expense

Salary Expense

PROBLEM 2-1 ___ , Continued

Automobile Expense

Blueprint Expense

Miscellaneous Expense

PROBLEM 2-1 ___, Concluded

3.

	Unadjusted Trial Balance					

PROBLEM 2-2 ___

1.

	DATE	DESCRIPTION	POST. REF.	DEBIT	CREDIT	
1						1
2						2
3						3
4						4
5						5
6						6
7						7
8						8
9						9
10						10
11						11
12						12
13						13
14						14
15						15
16						16
17						17
18						18
19						19
20						20
21						21
22						22
23						23
24						24
25						25
26						26
27						27
28						28
29						29
30						30
31						31
32						32
33						33
34						34
35						35
36						36

JOURNAL   PAGE

PROBLEM 2-2 ___, Continued

2.

Cash

Supplies

Accounts Payable

_____, *Capital*

_____, *Drawing*

Sales Commissions

PROBLEM 2-3 a

1.

			JOURNAL			PAGE 1		

	DATE 2008		DESCRIPTION	POST. REF.	DEBIT		CREDIT	
1	June	1	cash		18000—			1
2			B. Dodd, Capital				18000—	2
3								3
4		5	rent exp.		2150—			4
5			cash				2150—	5
6								6
7		6	equipment		8500—			7
8			account payable				8500—	8
9								9
10		8	truck		18000—			10
11			cash				10000—	11
12			note payable				8000—	12
13								13
14		10	supplies		1200—			14
15			Cash				1200—	15
16					10500—			16
17		12	cash				10500—	17
18			Fees earned					18
19								19
20		15	prepaid insurance exp.		2400—			20
21			cash				2400—	21
22								22
23		23	account receivable		5950—			23
24			Fees earned				5950—	24
25								25
26		24	truck exp.		1000—			26
27			cash				1000—	27
28								28
29		29	utilities exp.		1200—			29
30			cash				1200—	30
31								31
32		29	misc. exp.		400—			32
33			cash				400—	33
34								34
35		30	wages exp.		2900—			35
36			cash				2900—	36

PROBLEM 2-3 𝑎, Continued

JOURNAL   PAGE 2

	DATE	DESCRIPTION	POST. REF.	DEBIT	CREDIT	
1				2125—		1
2					2125—	2
3						3
4	30	Brooks Dodd, drawing		1750—		4
5		cash			1750—	5
6						6
7						7
8						8
9						9
10						10
11						11
12						12
13						13
14						14
15						15
16						16
17						17
18						18
19						19
20						20
21						21
22						22
23						23
24						24
25						25
26						26
27						27
28						28
29						29
30						30
31						31
32						32
33						33
34						34
35						35
36						36

PROBLEM 2-3 ___, Continued

2.

GENERAL LEDGER

ACCOUNT   *Cash*   ACCOUNT NO.   11

DATE	ITEM	POST. REF.	DEBIT	CREDIT	BALANCE DEBIT	BALANCE CREDIT

ACCOUNT   *Accounts Receivable*   ACCOUNT NO.   12

DATE	ITEM	POST. REF.	DEBIT	CREDIT	BALANCE DEBIT	BALANCE CREDIT

ACCOUNT   *Supplies*   ACCOUNT NO.   13

DATE	ITEM	POST. REF.	DEBIT	CREDIT	BALANCE DEBIT	BALANCE CREDIT

PROBLEM 2-3 ___, Continued

ACCOUNT   *Prepaid Insurance*   ACCOUNT NO.   14

DATE	ITEM	POST. REF.	DEBIT	CREDIT	BALANCE	
					DEBIT	CREDIT

ACCOUNT   *Equipment*   ACCOUNT NO.   16

DATE	ITEM	POST. REF.	DEBIT	CREDIT	BALANCE	
					DEBIT	CREDIT

ACCOUNT   *Truck*   ACCOUNT NO.   18

DATE	ITEM	POST. REF.	DEBIT	CREDIT	BALANCE	
					DEBIT	CREDIT

ACCOUNT   *Notes Payable*   ACCOUNT NO.   21

DATE	ITEM	POST. REF.	DEBIT	CREDIT	BALANCE	
					DEBIT	CREDIT

ACCOUNT   *Accounts Payable*   ACCOUNT NO.   22

DATE	ITEM	POST. REF.	DEBIT	CREDIT	BALANCE	
					DEBIT	CREDIT

PROBLEM 2-3 ___, Continued

ACCOUNT _____, *Capital* ACCOUNT NO. *31*

DATE	ITEM	POST. REF.	DEBIT	CREDIT	BALANCE DEBIT	BALANCE CREDIT

ACCOUNT _____, *Drawing* ACCOUNT NO. *32*

DATE	ITEM	POST. REF.	DEBIT	CREDIT	BALANCE DEBIT	BALANCE CREDIT

ACCOUNT *Fees Earned* ACCOUNT NO. *41*

DATE	ITEM	POST. REF.	DEBIT	CREDIT	BALANCE DEBIT	BALANCE CREDIT

PROBLEM 2-3 ___, Continued

ACCOUNT   *Wages Expense*   ACCOUNT NO.   51

DATE		ITEM	POST. REF.	DEBIT	CREDIT	BALANCE	
						DEBIT	CREDIT

ACCOUNT   *Rent Expense*   ACCOUNT NO.   53

DATE		ITEM	POST. REF.	DEBIT	CREDIT	BALANCE	
						DEBIT	CREDIT

ACCOUNT   *Utilities Expense*   ACCOUNT NO.   54

DATE		ITEM	POST. REF.	DEBIT	CREDIT	BALANCE	
						DEBIT	CREDIT

ACCOUNT   *Truck Expense*   ACCOUNT NO.   55

DATE		ITEM	POST. REF.	DEBIT	CREDIT	BALANCE	
						DEBIT	CREDIT

ACCOUNT   *Miscellaneous Expenses*   ACCOUNT NO.   59

DATE		ITEM	POST. REF.	DEBIT	CREDIT	BALANCE	
						DEBIT	CREDIT

PROBLEM 2-3 ___ , Concluded

3.

Unadjusted Trial Balance

This Page Not Used.

PROBLEM 2-4 ___, Continued

1. and 3.

ACCOUNT   *Cash*   ACCOUNT NO.   11

DATE	ITEM	POST. REF.	DEBIT	CREDIT	BALANCE DEBIT	BALANCE CREDIT

ACCOUNT   *Accounts Receivable*   ACCOUNT NO.   12

DATE	ITEM	POST. REF.	DEBIT	CREDIT	BALANCE DEBIT	BALANCE CREDIT

ACCOUNT   *Prepaid Insurance*   ACCOUNT NO.   13

DATE	ITEM	POST. REF.	DEBIT	CREDIT	BALANCE DEBIT	BALANCE CREDIT

PROBLEM 2-4 ___ , Continued

ACCOUNT   *Office Supplies*   ACCOUNT NO.   14

DATE		ITEM	POST. REF.	DEBIT	CREDIT	BALANCE	
						DEBIT	CREDIT

ACCOUNT   *Land*   ACCOUNT NO.   16

DATE		ITEM	POST. REF.	DEBIT	CREDIT	BALANCE	
						DEBIT	CREDIT

ACCOUNT   *Accounts Payable*   ACCOUNT NO.   21

DATE		ITEM	POST. REF.	DEBIT	CREDIT	BALANCE	
						DEBIT	CREDIT

ACCOUNT   *Unearned Rent*   ACCOUNT NO.   22

DATE		ITEM	POST. REF.	DEBIT	CREDIT	BALANCE	
						DEBIT	CREDIT

ACCOUNT   *Notes Payable*   ACCOUNT NO.   23

DATE		ITEM	POST. REF.	DEBIT	CREDIT	BALANCE	
						DEBIT	CREDIT

PROBLEM 2-4 ___, Continued

ACCOUNT _____, *Capital*   ACCOUNT NO.   31

DATE	ITEM	POST. REF.	DEBIT	CREDIT	BALANCE	
					DEBIT	CREDIT

ACCOUNT _____, *Drawing*   ACCOUNT NO.   32

DATE	ITEM	POST. REF.	DEBIT	CREDIT	BALANCE	
					DEBIT	CREDIT

ACCOUNT   *Fees Earned*   ACCOUNT NO.   41

DATE	ITEM	POST. REF.	DEBIT	CREDIT	BALANCE	
					DEBIT	CREDIT

ACCOUNT   *Salary and Commission Expense*   ACCOUNT NO.   51

DATE	ITEM	POST. REF.	DEBIT	CREDIT	BALANCE	
					DEBIT	CREDIT

PROBLEM 2-4 ___, Continued

ACCOUNT   *Rent Expense*   ACCOUNT NO. *52*

DATE	ITEM	POST. REF.	DEBIT	CREDIT	BALANCE DEBIT	BALANCE CREDIT

ACCOUNT   *Advertising Expense*   ACCOUNT NO. *53*

DATE	ITEM	POST. REF.	DEBIT	CREDIT	BALANCE DEBIT	BALANCE CREDIT

ACCOUNT   *Automobile Expense*   ACCOUNT NO. *54*

DATE	ITEM	POST. REF.	DEBIT	CREDIT	BALANCE DEBIT	BALANCE CREDIT

ACCOUNT   *Miscellaneous Expense*   ACCOUNT NO. *59*

DATE	ITEM	POST. REF.	DEBIT	CREDIT	BALANCE DEBIT	BALANCE CREDIT

PROBLEM 2-4 ___ , Concluded

4.

Unadjusted Trial Balance						

This Page Not Used.

PROBLEM 2-5 ___

JOURNAL

	DATE		DESCRIPTION	POST. REF.	DEBIT	CREDIT	
1	20— July	1	Rent Expense	52	1 5 4 0 00		1
2			Cash	11		1 5 4 0 00	2
3							3
4		4	Supplies	12	1 4 9 00		4
5			Accounts Payable	22		1 4 9 00	5
6							6
7		6	Advertising Expense	54	2 7 5 00		7
8			Cash	11		2 7 5 00	8
9							9
10		8	Cash	11	1 5 9 5 30		10
11			Service Revenue	41		1 5 9 5 30	11
12							12
13		9	Prepaid Insurance	13	1 4 4 00		13
14			Cash	11		1 4 4 00	14
15							15
16		10	Land	16	1 2 0 0 0 00		16
17			Cash	11		5 5 0 0 00	17
18			Notes Payable	21		6 5 0 0 00	18
19							19
20		13	Accounts Payable	22	8 4 7 20		20
21			Cash	11		8 4 7 20	21
22							22
23		14	Miscellaneous Expense	58	1 6 2 10		23
24			Cash	11		1 6 2 10	24
25							25
26		15	Wages Expense	51	1 1 2 8 60		26
27			Cash	11		1 1 2 8 60	27
28							28
29		15	Cash	11	1 7 8 5 50		29
30			Service Revenue	41		1 7 8 5 50	30
31							31
32		16	Martin Tresp, Drawing	32	7 5 0 00		32
33			Cash	11		7 5 0 00	33
34							34
35		17	Supplies	12	2 1 2 60		35
36			Accounts Payable	22		2 1 2 60	36

PROBLEM 2-5 ___, Continued

JOURNAL

	DATE		DESCRIPTION	POST. REF.	DEBIT	CREDIT	
1	20— July	20	Cash	11	1 6 6 2 20		1
2			Service Revenue	41		1 6 6 2 20	2
3							3
4		22	Accounts Payable	22	7 4 20		4
5			Supplies	12		7 4 20	5
6							6
7		25	Miscellaneous Expense	58	1 2 1 40		7
8			Cash	11		1 2 1 40	8
9							9
10		25	Cash	11	1 6 8 1 30		10
11			Service Revenue	41		1 6 8 1 30	11
12							12
13		30	Utilities Expense	53	4 3 6 60		13
14			Cash	11		4 3 6 60	14
15							15
16		31	Wages Expense	51	1 3 9 0 00		16
17			Cash	11		1 3 9 0 00	17
18							18
19		31	Martin Tresp, Drawing	32	6 0 0 00		19
20			Cash	11		6 0 0 00	20
21							21
22		31	Cash	11	1 2 7 6 10		22
23			Service Revenue	41		1 2 7 6 10	23
24							24
25							25
26							26
27							27
28							28
29							29
30							30
31							31
32							32
33							33
34							34
35							35
36							36

PROBLEM 2-5 ___, Continued

1. and 3.

ACCOUNT *Cash*   ACCOUNT NO. 11

DATE		ITEM	POST. REF.	DEBIT	CREDIT	BALANCE DEBIT	BALANCE CREDIT
20— July	1	Balance	√			13 810 50	
	1		19		1 540 00		
	6		19		275 00		
	8		19	1 595 30			
	9		19		144 00		
	10		19		5 500 00		
	13		19		847 20		
	14		19		162 10		
	15		19		1 128 60		
	15		19	1 785 50			
	16		19		750 00		
	20		20	1 662 20			
	25		20		121 40		
	25		20	1 683 30			
	30		20		436 60		
	31		20		1 390 00		
	31		20		600 00		
	31		20	1 276 10		8 917 80	

ACCOUNT *Supplies*   ACCOUNT NO. 12

DATE		ITEM	POST. REF.	DEBIT	CREDIT	BALANCE DEBIT	BALANCE CREDIT
20— July	1	Balance	√			710 50	
	4		19	149 00			
	17		19	212 60			
	22		20		74 20	997 90	

ACCOUNT *Prepaid Insurance*   ACCOUNT NO. 13

DATE		ITEM	POST. REF.	DEBIT	CREDIT	BALANCE DEBIT	BALANCE CREDIT
20— July	1	Balance	√			251 50	
	9		19	1 440 00		1 691 50	

PROBLEM 2-5 ___ , Continued

ACCOUNT   *Land*   ACCOUNT NO.   16

DATE		ITEM	POST. REF.	DEBIT	CREDIT	BALANCE DEBIT	BALANCE CREDIT
20—July	1	Balance	√	14 625 00		14 625 00	
	10		19	1 200 00		15 825 00	

ACCOUNT   *Notes Payable*   ACCOUNT NO.   21

DATE		ITEM	POST. REF.	DEBIT	CREDIT	BALANCE DEBIT	BALANCE CREDIT
20—July	10		19		6 500 00		6 500 00

ACCOUNT   *Accounts Payable*   ACCOUNT NO.   22

DATE		ITEM	POST. REF.	DEBIT	CREDIT	BALANCE DEBIT	BALANCE CREDIT
20—July	1	Balance	√				1 637 30
	4		19		1 49 00		
	13		19	8 47 20			
	17		19		2 12 60		
	22		20	7 4 20			1 225 90

ACCOUNT   *Martin Tresp, Capital*   ACCOUNT NO.   31

DATE		ITEM	POST. REF.	DEBIT	CREDIT	BALANCE DEBIT	BALANCE CREDIT
20—July	1	Balance	√				27 760 20

PROBLEM 2-5 ___, Continued

ACCOUNT   *Martin Tresp, Drawing*   ACCOUNT NO.   *32*

DATE		ITEM	POST. REF.	DEBIT	CREDIT	BALANCE DEBIT	BALANCE CREDIT
20— July	16		19	7 5 0 00			
	31		20	6 0 0 00		1 3 5 0 00	

ACCOUNT   *Service Revenue*   ACCOUNT NO.   *41*

DATE		ITEM	POST. REF.	DEBIT	CREDIT	BALANCE DEBIT	BALANCE CREDIT
20— July	8		19		1 5 9 5 30		
	15		19		1 7 8 5 50		
	20		20		1 6 6 2 20		
	25		20		1 6 8 1 30		
	31		20		1 2 7 6 10		8 0 0 0 40

ACCOUNT   *Wages Expense*   ACCOUNT NO.   *51*

DATE		ITEM	POST. REF.	DEBIT	CREDIT	BALANCE DEBIT	BALANCE CREDIT
20— July	15		19	1 1 2 8 60			
	31		20	1 9 3 0 00		3 0 5 8 60	

PROBLEM 2-5 ___, Continued

ACCOUNT   *Rent Expense*   ACCOUNT NO.   52

DATE		ITEM	POST. REF.	DEBIT	CREDIT	BALANCE DEBIT	BALANCE CREDIT
20— July	1		19	1 5 4 0 00		1 5 4 0 00	

ACCOUNT   *Utilities Expense*   ACCOUNT NO.   53

DATE		ITEM	POST. REF.	DEBIT	CREDIT	BALANCE DEBIT	BALANCE CREDIT
20— July	30		20	4 3 6 60		4 3 6 60	

ACCOUNT   *Advertising Expense*   ACCOUNT NO.   54

DATE		ITEM	POST. REF.	DEBIT	CREDIT	BALANCE DEBIT	BALANCE CREDIT
20— July	6		19	2 7 5 00		2 7 5 00	

ACCOUNT   *Miscellaneous Expense*   ACCOUNT NO.   58

DATE		ITEM	POST. REF.	DEBIT	CREDIT	BALANCE DEBIT	BALANCE CREDIT
20— July	14		19	1 6 2 10		1 6 2 10	
	25		20	1 2 1 40		2 8 3 50	

PROBLEM 2-5 ___ , Continued

MAINSTAY TV REPAIR
Unadjusted Trial Balance
July 31, 20—

Cash	8 9 1 7 80	
Supplies	9 7 9 90	
Prepaid Insurance	1 6 9 1 50	
Land	1 5 8 2 5 00	
Notes Payable	6 5 0 0 00	
Accounts Payable		1 2 2 5 90
Martin Tresp, Capital		2 7 7 6 0 20
Martin Tresp, Drawing		1 3 5 0 00
Service Revenue		8 0 0 0 40
Wages Expense	3 0 5 8 60	
Rent Expense	4 3 6 60	
Utilities Expense	1 5 4 0 00	
Advertising Expense	2 7 5 00	
	3 9 2 2 4 40	3 8 3 3 6 50

This Page Not Used.

PROBLEM 2-5 ___, Concluded

Verification Schedule

1. Totals of preliminary trial balance: Debit $ _____

                                                      Credit $ _____

2. Difference between preliminary trial balance totals: $ _____

3. Errors in trial balance:

_____

_____

_____

_____

_____

_____

4. Errors in account balances:

_____

_____

5. Errors in posting:

_____

_____

_____

_____

_____

_____

_____

_____

6. Journal entry:

JOURNAL   PAGE *19*

	DATE		DESCRIPTION	POST. REF.	DEBIT	CREDIT	
1							1
2							2
3							3
4							4

7.

MAINSTAY TV REPAIR
Unadjusted Trial Balance
July 31, 20—

PROBLEM 2-6 ___

1.

	Debit Balances	Credit Balances
Cash		
Accounts Receivable		
Supplies		
Prepaid Insurance		
Equipment		
Notes Payable		
Accounts Payable		
_____, Capital		
_____, Drawing		
Fees Earned		
Wages Expense		
Rent Expense		
Advertising Expense		
Gas, Electricity, and Water Expense		
Miscellaneous Expense		

Corrected Unadjusted Trial Balance

2.

This Page Not Used.

CONTINUING PROBLEM

2. and 3.

JOURNAL

PAGE *1*

	DATE		DESCRIPTION	POST. REF.	DEBIT	CREDIT	
1							1
2							2
3							3
4							4
5							5
6							6
7							7
8							8
9							9
10							10
11							11
12							12
13							13
14							14
15							15
16							16
17							17
18							18
19							19
20							20
21							21
22							22
23							23
24							24
25							25
26							26
27							27
28							28
29							29
30							30
31							31
32							32
33							33
34							34
35							35
36							36

CONTINUING PROBLEM, Continued

JOURNAL

	DATE	DESCRIPTION	POST. REF.	DEBIT	CREDIT	
1						1
2						2
3						3
4						4
5						5
6						6
7						7
8						8
9						9
10						10
11						11
12						12
13						13
14						14
15						15
16						16
17						17
18						18
19						19
20						20
21						21
22						22
23						23
24						24
25						25
26						26
27						27
28						28
29						29
30						30
31						31
32						32
33						33
34						34
35						35
36						36

CONTINUING PROBLEM, **Continued**

1. and 3.

ACCOUNT   *Cash*   ACCOUNT NO.   *11*

DATE		ITEM	POST. REF.	DEBIT	CREDIT	BALANCE	
						DEBIT	CREDIT

ACCOUNT   *Accounts Receivable*   ACCOUNT NO.   *12*

DATE		ITEM	POST. REF.	DEBIT	CREDIT	BALANCE	
						DEBIT	CREDIT

CONTINUING PROBLEM, Continued

ACCOUNT *Supplies*   ACCOUNT NO. *14*

DATE	ITEM	POST. REF.	DEBIT	CREDIT	BALANCE DEBIT	BALANCE CREDIT

ACCOUNT *Prepaid Insurance*   ACCOUNT NO. *15*

DATE	ITEM	POST. REF.	DEBIT	CREDIT	BALANCE DEBIT	BALANCE CREDIT

ACCOUNT *Office Equipment*   ACCOUNT NO. *17*

DATE	ITEM	POST. REF.	DEBIT	CREDIT	BALANCE DEBIT	BALANCE CREDIT

ACCOUNT *Accumulated Depreciation—Office Equipment*   ACCOUNT NO. *18*

DATE	ITEM	POST. REF.	DEBIT	CREDIT	BALANCE DEBIT	BALANCE CREDIT

ACCOUNT *Accounts Payable*   ACCOUNT NO. *21*

DATE	ITEM	POST. REF.	DEBIT	CREDIT	BALANCE DEBIT	BALANCE CREDIT

CONTINUING PROBLEM, Continued

ACCOUNT   *Wages Payable*   ACCOUNT NO.   22

DATE	ITEM	POST. REF.	DEBIT	CREDIT	BALANCE	
					DEBIT	CREDIT

ACCOUNT   *Unearned Revenue*   ACCOUNT NO.   23

DATE	ITEM	POST. REF.	DEBIT	CREDIT	BALANCE	
					DEBIT	CREDIT

ACCOUNT   *Kris Payne, Capital*   ACCOUNT NO.   31

DATE	ITEM	POST. REF.	DEBIT	CREDIT	BALANCE	
					DEBIT	CREDIT

ACCOUNT   *Kris Payne, Drawing*   ACCOUNT NO.   32

DATE	ITEM	POST. REF.	DEBIT	CREDIT	BALANCE	
					DEBIT	CREDIT

ACCOUNT   *Account Summary*   ACCOUNT NO.   33

DATE	ITEM	POST. REF.	DEBIT	CREDIT	BALANCE	
					DEBIT	CREDIT

CONTINUING PROBLEM, Continued

ACCOUNT   *Fees Earned*   ACCOUNT NO.   41

DATE	ITEM	POST. REF.	DEBIT	CREDIT	BALANCE DEBIT	BALANCE CREDIT

ACCOUNT   *Wages Expense*   ACCOUNT NO.   50

DATE	ITEM	POST. REF.	DEBIT	CREDIT	BALANCE DEBIT	BALANCE CREDIT

ACCOUNT   *Office Rent Expense*   ACCOUNT NO.   51

DATE	ITEM	POST. REF.	DEBIT	CREDIT	BALANCE DEBIT	BALANCE CREDIT

ACCOUNT   *Equipment Rent Expense*   ACCOUNT NO.   52

DATE	ITEM	POST. REF.	DEBIT	CREDIT	BALANCE DEBIT	BALANCE CREDIT

CONTINUING PROBLEM, Continued

ACCOUNT   *Utilities Expense*   ACCOUNT NO.   53

DATE		ITEM	POST. REF.	DEBIT	CREDIT	BALANCE	
						DEBIT	CREDIT

ACCOUNT   *Music Expense*   ACCOUNT NO.   54

DATE		ITEM	POST. REF.	DEBIT	CREDIT	BALANCE	
						DEBIT	CREDIT

ACCOUNT   *Advertising Expense*   ACCOUNT NO.   55

DATE		ITEM	POST. REF.	DEBIT	CREDIT	BALANCE	
						DEBIT	CREDIT

ACCOUNT   *Supplies Expense*   ACCOUNT NO.   56

DATE		ITEM	POST. REF.	DEBIT	CREDIT	BALANCE	
						DEBIT	CREDIT

ACCOUNT   *Depreciation Expense*   ACCOUNT NO.   58

DATE		ITEM	POST. REF.	DEBIT	CREDIT	BALANCE	
						DEBIT	CREDIT

CONTINUING PROBLEM, Concluded

ACCOUNT	*Miscellaneous Expense*				ACCOUNT NO.	59

DATE	ITEM	POST. REF.	DEBIT	CREDIT	BALANCE DEBIT	BALANCE CREDIT

4.

Unadjusted Trial Balance

EXERCISE 3-1

1. Fees earned but not yet received: _____

2. Taxes owed but payable in the following period: _____

3. Utilities owed but not yet paid: _____

4. Salary owed but not yet paid: _____

5. Supplies on hand: _____

6. Fees received but not yet earned: _____

7. A two-year premium paid on a fire insurance policy: _____

8. Subscriptions received in advance by a magazine publisher: _____

EXERCISE 3-2

Account	Answer
Accounts Receivable	Normally requires adjustment (AR).
Cash..	
Charmaine Hollis, Drawing	
Interest Payable........................	
Interest Receivable...................	
Land	
Office Equipment	
Prepaid Rent.............................	
Supplies	
Unearned Fees.........................	
Wages Expense........................	

EXERCISE 3-3

JOURNAL   PAGE

	DATE		DESCRIPTION	POST. REF.	DEBIT	CREDIT	
1							1
2							2
3							3

EXERCISE 3-4

_____

_____

EXERCISE 3-5

a. _____

_____

_____

b. _____

_____

_____

EXERCISE 3-6

a. and b.

JOURNAL   PAGE

	DATE		DESCRIPTION	POST. REF.	DEBIT	CREDIT	
1							1
2							2
3							3
4							4
5							5
6							6

EXERCISE 3-7

a. and b.

JOURNAL   PAGE

	DATE		DESCRIPTION	POST. REF.	DEBIT	CREDIT	
1							1
2							2
3							3
4							4
5							5
6							6

EXERCISE 3-8

JOURNAL   PAGE

	DATE		DESCRIPTION	POST. REF.	DEBIT	CREDIT	
1							1
2							2
3							3

EXERCISE 3-9

a. _____

_____

_____

b. _____

_____

_____

EXERCISE 3-10

a. and b.

JOURNAL   PAGE

	DATE		DESCRIPTION	POST. REF.	DEBIT	CREDIT	
1							1
2							2
3							3

b. _____

_____

EXERCISE 3-11

a. and b.

JOURNAL   PAGE

	DATE		DESCRIPTION	POST. REF.	DEBIT	CREDIT	
1							1
2							2
3							3
4							4
5							5
6							6
7							7

EXERCISE 3-12

a. _____

_____

b. _____

_____

EXERCISE 3-13

a. and b.

JOURNAL   PAGE

	DATE		DESCRIPTION	POST. REF.	DEBIT	CREDIT	
1							1
2							2
3							3
4							4
5							5
6							6
7							7

EXERCISE 3-14

_____

_____

_____

EXERCISE 3-15

a. _____

_____

_____

_____

b. _____

_____

_____

_____

EXERCISE 3-16

a. _____

_____

b. _____

_____

_____

EXERCISE 3-17

a.

JOURNAL   PAGE

	DATE		DESCRIPTION	POST. REF.	DEBIT	CREDIT	
1							1
2							2
3							3
4							4
5							5
6							6
7							7

b. _____

EXERCISE 3-18

JOURNAL   PAGE

	DATE		DESCRIPTION	POST. REF.	DEBIT	CREDIT	
1							1
2							2
3							3
4							4
5							5
6							6
7							7

EXERCISE 3-19

a. _____

b. _____

_____

EXERCISE 3-20

a. _____

b. _____

_____

EXERCISE 3-21

_____

EXERCISE 3-22

a. _____

b. _____

EXERCISE 3-23

	Error (a)		Error (b)	
	Overstated	**Understated**	**Overstated**	**Understated**
1. Revenue for the year would be.........................	$	$	$	$
2. Expenses for the year would be	$	$	$	$
3. Net income for the year would be....................	$	$	$	$
4. Assets at August 31 would be	$	$	$	$
5. Liabilities at August 31 would be	$	$	$	$
6. Owner's equity at August 31 would be	$	$	$	$

EXERCISE 3-24

_____

EXERCISE 3-25

a.

JOURNAL   PAGE

	DATE		DESCRIPTION	POST. REF.	DEBIT	CREDIT	
1							1
2							2
3							3

EXERCISE 3-25 (Continued)

b. (1) _____

_____

_____

(2) _____

_____

_____

EXERCISE 3-26

JOURNAL   PAGE _____

	DATE		DESCRIPTION	POST. REF.	DEBIT	CREDIT	
1							1
2							2
3							3
4							4
5							5
6							6
7							7
8							8
9							9
10							10
11							11
12							12
13							13
14							14

EXERCISE 3-27

EXERCISE 3-27 Concluded

Adjusted Trial Balance (concluded)					

This Page Not Used.

PROBLEM 3-2 ___

		JOURNAL			PAGE

	DATE	DESCRIPTION	POST. REF.	DEBIT	CREDIT	
1						1
2						2
3						3
4						4
5						5
6						6
7						7
8						8
9						9
10						10
11						11
12						12
13						13
14						14
15						15
16						16
17						17
18						18
19						19
20						20
21						21
22						22
23						23
24						24
25						25
26						26
27						27
28						28
29						29
30						30
31						31
32						32
33						33
34						34
35						35
36						36

106

This Page Not Used.

PROBLEM 3-4 ___

JOURNAL

PAGE ____

	DATE		DESCRIPTION	POST. REF.	DEBIT	CREDIT	
1							1
2							2
3							3
4							4
5							5
6							6
7							7
8							8
9							9
10							10
11							11
12							12
13							13
14							14
15							15
16							16
17							17
18							18
19							19
20							20
21							21
22							22
23							23
24							24
25							25
26							26
27							27
28							28
29							29
30							30
31							31
32							32
33							33
34							34
35							35
36							36

This Page Not Used.

PROBLEM 3-6 ___

1.

JOURNAL

PAGE

	DATE		DESCRIPTION	POST. REF.	DEBIT	CREDIT	
1							1
2							2
3							3
4							4
5							5
6							6
7							7
8							8
9							9
10							10
11							11
12							12
13							13
14							14
15							15
16							16
17							17
18							18
19							19
20							20
21							21
22							22
23							23
24							24
25							25
26							26
27							27
28							28
29							29
30							30
31							31
32							32
33							33
34							34
35							35
36							36

PROBLEM 3-6 ___, Concluded

2.

	Net Income	Total Assets	Total Liabilities	Total Owner's Equity
Reported amounts	$ _____	$ _____	$ _____	$ _____
Corrections:				
Adjustment (a)	_____	_____	_____	_____
Adjustment (b)	_____	_____	_____	_____
Adjustment (c)	_____	_____	_____	_____
Adjustment (d)	_____	_____	_____	_____
Corrected amounts	$ _____	$ _____	$ _____	$ _____

CONTINUING PROBLEM

1.

JOURNAL

PAGE 3

	DATE		DESCRIPTION	POST. REF.	DEBIT	CREDIT	
1							1
2							2
3							3
4							4
5							5
6							6
7							7
8							8
9							9
10							10
11							11
12							12
13							13
14							14
15							15
16							16
17							17
18							18
19							19
20							20
21							21
22							22
23							23
24							24
25							25
26							26
27							27
28							28
29							29
30							30
31							31
32							32
33							33
34							34
35							35
36							36

CONTINUING PROBLEM, Continued

2.

ACCOUNT   *Cash*   ACCOUNT NO.   11

DATE	ITEM	POST. REF.	DEBIT	CREDIT	BALANCE DEBIT	CREDIT

ACCOUNT   *Accounts Receivable*   ACCOUNT NO.   12

DATE	ITEM	POST. REF.	DEBIT	CREDIT	BALANCE DEBIT	CREDIT

ACCOUNT   *Supplies*   ACCOUNT NO.   *14*

DATE		ITEM	POST. REF.	DEBIT	CREDIT	BALANCE	
						DEBIT	CREDIT

ACCOUNT   *Prepaid Insurance*   ACCOUNT NO.   *15*

DATE		ITEM	POST. REF.	DEBIT	CREDIT	BALANCE	
						DEBIT	CREDIT

ACCOUNT   *Office Equipment*   ACCOUNT NO.   *17*

DATE		ITEM	POST. REF.	DEBIT	CREDIT	BALANCE	
						DEBIT	CREDIT

ACCOUNT   *Accumulated Depreciation—Office Equipment*   ACCOUNT NO.   *18*

DATE		ITEM	POST. REF.	DEBIT	CREDIT	BALANCE	
						DEBIT	CREDIT

ACCOUNT   *Accounts Payable*   ACCOUNT NO.   *21*

DATE		ITEM	POST. REF.	DEBIT	CREDIT	BALANCE	
						DEBIT	CREDIT

CONTINUING PROBLEM, Continued

ACCOUNT　　*Wages Payable*　　　　ACCOUNT NO.　22

DATE	ITEM	POST. REF.	DEBIT	CREDIT	BALANCE DEBIT	BALANCE CREDIT

ACCOUNT　　*Unearned Revenue*　　　　ACCOUNT NO.　23

DATE	ITEM	POST. REF.	DEBIT	CREDIT	BALANCE DEBIT	BALANCE CREDIT

ACCOUNT　　*Kris Payne, Capital*　　　　ACCOUNT NO.　31

DATE	ITEM	POST. REF.	DEBIT	CREDIT	BALANCE DEBIT	BALANCE CREDIT

ACCOUNT　　*Kris Payne, Drawing*　　　　ACCOUNT NO.　32

DATE	ITEM	POST. REF.	DEBIT	CREDIT	BALANCE DEBIT	BALANCE CREDIT

ACCOUNT　　*Income Summary*　　　　ACCOUNT NO.　33

DATE	ITEM	POST. REF.	DEBIT	CREDIT	BALANCE DEBIT	BALANCE CREDIT

Name _____

CONTINUING PROBLEM, Continued

ACCOUNT   *Fees Earned*   ACCOUNT NO.   41

DATE		ITEM	POST. REF.	DEBIT	CREDIT	BALANCE DEBIT	CREDIT

ACCOUNT   *Wages Expense*   ACCOUNT NO.   50

DATE		ITEM	POST. REF.	DEBIT	CREDIT	BALANCE DEBIT	CREDIT

ACCOUNT   *Office Rent Expense*   ACCOUNT NO.   51

DATE		ITEM	POST. REF.	DEBIT	CREDIT	BALANCE DEBIT	CREDIT

ACCOUNT   *Equipment Rent Expense*   ACCOUNT NO.   52

DATE		ITEM	POST. REF.	DEBIT	CREDIT	BALANCE DEBIT	CREDIT

CONTINUING PROBLEM, Continued

ACCOUNT   *Utilities Expense*   ACCOUNT NO.   53

DATE	ITEM	POST. REF.	DEBIT	CREDIT	BALANCE DEBIT	BALANCE CREDIT

ACCOUNT   *Music Expense*   ACCOUNT NO.   54

DATE	ITEM	POST. REF.	DEBIT	CREDIT	BALANCE DEBIT	BALANCE CREDIT

ACCOUNT   *Advertising Expense*   ACCOUNT NO.   55

DATE	ITEM	POST. REF.	DEBIT	CREDIT	BALANCE DEBIT	BALANCE CREDIT

ACCOUNT   *Supplies Expense*   ACCOUNT NO.   56

DATE	ITEM	POST. REF.	DEBIT	CREDIT	BALANCE DEBIT	BALANCE CREDIT

ACCOUNT   *Insurance Expense*   ACCOUNT NO.   57

DATE	ITEM	POST. REF.	DEBIT	CREDIT	BALANCE DEBIT	BALANCE CREDIT

ACCOUNT   *Depreciation Expense*   ACCOUNT NO.   58

DATE	ITEM	POST. REF.	DEBIT	CREDIT	BALANCE DEBIT	BALANCE CREDIT

ACCOUNT   *Miscellaneous Expense*   ACCOUNT NO.   59

DATE	ITEM	POST. REF.	DEBIT	CREDIT	BALANCE DEBIT	BALANCE CREDIT

CONTINUING PROBLEM, Concluded

3.

	Adjusted Trial Balance		

EXERCISE 4-1

1. Accounts Payable: _____
2. Accounts Receivable: _____
3. Beth Posey, Capital: _____
4. Beth Posey, Drawing: _____
5. Fees Earned: _____
6. Supplies: _____
7. Unearned Fees: _____
8. Utilities Expense: _____
9. Wages Expense: _____
10. Wages Payable: _____

EXERCISE 4-2

1. Accounts Receivable: _____
2. Fees Earned: _____
3. Insurance Expense: _____
4. Land: _____
5. Prepaid Advertising: _____
6. Prepaid Insurance: _____
7. Rent Revenue: _____
8. Salary Expense: _____
9. Salary Payable: _____
10. Supplies: _____
11. Supplies Expense: _____
12. Unearned Rent: _____

EXERCISE 4-3

Income Statement

Statement of Owner's Equity

Name _____

Chapter 4

EXERCISE 4-3, Concluded

Balance Sheet

EXERCISE   4-4

Income Statement

Statement of Owner's Equity

Name _____

Chapter 4

EXERCISE 4-4, Concluded

Balance Sheet

EXERCISE 4-5

Income Statement

EXERCISE 4-6

Income Statement

EXERCISE   4-7

a.

	Income Statement								

b. _____

_____

_____

_____

_____

EXERCISE 4-8

	Statement of Owner's Equity								

EXERCISE 4-9

Statement of Owner's Equity							

EXERCISE 4-10

1. Accounts receivable: _____

2. Building: _____

3. Cash: _____

4. Equipment: _____

5. Prepaid insurance: _____

6. Supplies: _____

EXERCISE 4-11

_____

_____

_____

_____

_____

_____

_____

_____

_____

_____

_____

_____

_____

_____

_____

Name _____

EXERCISE 4-12

Balance Sheet

EXERCISE 4-13

Name _____

EXERCISE 4-13, Concluded

Balance Sheet

Chapter 4

EXERCISE 4-14

a. Accounts Receivable: _____

b. Accumulated Depreciation—Equipment: _____

c. Depreciation Expense—Equipment: _____

d. Equipment: _____

e. Fees Earned: _____

f. Keri Upshaw, Capital: _____

g. Keri Upshaw, Drawing: _____

h. Land: _____

i. Supplies: _____

j. Supplies Expense: _____

k. Wages Expense: _____

l. Wages Payable: _____

EXERCISE 4-15

_____

_____

_____

_____

_____

_____

_____

_____

EXERCISE 4-16

a.

JOURNAL   PAGE

	DATE		DESCRIPTION	POST. REF.	DEBIT	CREDIT	
1							1
2							2
3							3
4							4
5							5
6							6

b. _____

EXERCISE 4-17

JOURNAL   PAGE

	DATE		DESCRIPTION	POST. REF.	DEBIT	CREDIT	
1							1
2							2
3							3
4							4
5							5
6							6
7							7
8							8
9							9
10							10
11							11
12							12
13							13
14							14

EXERCISE 4-18

a. Accounts payable: _____

b. Accumulated Depreciation: _____

c. Cash: _____

d. Depreciation Expense: _____

e. Fees Earned: _____

f. Office Equipment: _____

g. Salaries Expense: _____

h. Salaries Payable: _____

i. Stephanie Hamm, Capital: _____

j. Stephanie Hamm, Drawing: _____

k. Supplies: _____

EXERCISE 4-19

Post-Closing Trial Balance

EXERCISE 4-20

1. _____   6. _____
2. _____   7. _____
3. _____   8. _____
4. _____   9. _____
5. _____   10. _____

EXERCISE 4-21

1. _____   6. _____
2. _____   7. _____
3. _____   8. _____
4. _____   9. _____
5. _____   10. _____

EXERCISE 4-22

Dakota Services Co.
End-of-Period Spreadsheet (Work Sheet)
For the Year Ended January 31, 2008

	Unadjusted Trial Balance		Adjustments		Adjusted Trial Balance		Income Statement		Balance Sheet		
Account Title	Dr.	Cr.	Dr.	Cr.	Dr.	Cr.	Dr.	Cr.	Dr.	Cr.	
1 Cash	4										1
2 Accounts Receivable	25										2
3 Supplies	4										3
4 Prepaid Insurance	6										4
5 Land	25										5
6 Equipment	16										6
7 Accumulated Depr—Equip.		1									7
8 Accounts Payable		13									8
9 Wages Payable		0									9
10 Christina Keene, Capital		56									10
11 Christina Keene, Drawing	4										11
12 Fees Earned		30									12
13 Wages Expense	8										13
14 Rent Expense	4										14
15 Insurance Expense	0										15
16 Utilities Expense	3										16
17 Depreciation Expense	0										17
18 Supplies Expense	0										18
19 Miscellaneous Expense	1										19
20 Totals											20
21											21
22											22

EXERCISE 4-23

Dakota Services Co.
End-of-Period Spreadsheet (Work Sheet)
For the Year Ended January 31, 2008

	Account Title	Unadjusted Trial Balance Dr.	Cr.	Adjustments Dr.	Cr.	Adjusted Trial Balance Dr.	Cr.	Income Statement Dr.	Cr.	Balance Sheet Dr.	Cr.	
1	Cash					4						1
2	Accounts Receivable					30						2
3	Supplies					1						3
4	Prepaid Insurance					2						4
5	Land					25						5
6	Equipment					16						6
7	Accumulated Depr—Equip.						1					7
8	Accounts Payable						13					8
9	Wages Payable						0					9
10	Christina Keene, Capital						56					10
11	Christina Keene, Drawing					4						11
12	Fees Earned						35					12
13	Wages Expense					9						13
14	Rent Expense					4						14
15	Insurance Expense					4						15
16	Utilities Expense					3						16
17	Depreciation Expense					2						17
18	Supplies Expense					3						18
19	Miscellaneous Expense					1						19
20	Totals					108	108					20
21												21
22												22

EXERCISE 4-24

Income Statement

Statement of Owner's Equity

Name _____

Chapter 4

EXERCISE 4-24, Concluded

Balance Sheet

EXERCISE 4-25

JOURNAL

PAGE

	DATE		DESCRIPTION	POST. REF.	DEBIT	CREDIT	
1							1
2							2
3							3
4							4
5							5
6							6
7							7
8							8
9							9
10							10
11							11
12							12
13							13
14							14
15							15
16							16
17							17
18							18
19							19

EXERCISE 4-26

JOURNAL

	DATE		DESCRIPTION	POST. REF.	DEBIT	CREDIT	
1							1
2							2
3							3
4							4
5							5
6							6
7							7
8							8
9							9
10							10
11							11
12							12
13							13
14							14
15							15
16							16
17							17

144

This Page Not Used.

PROBLEM 4-1 ___

. Omit "00" in the cents columns.

Income Statement

. Omit "00" in the cents columns.

Statement of Owner's Equity

Name _____

PROBLEM 4-1 ____, Continued

3. *Omit "00" in the cents columns.*

Balance Sheet

PROBLEM 4-1 ___, Continued

JOURNAL

PAGE _____

	DATE		DESCRIPTION	POST. REF.	DEBIT	CREDIT	
1							1
2							2
3							3
4							4
5							5
6							6
7							7
8							8
9							9
10							10
11							11
12							12
13							13
14							14
15							15
16							16
17							17
18							18
19							19
20							20
21							21
22							22
23							23
24							24
25							25
26							26
27							27
28							28
29							29
30							30
31							31
32							32
33							33
34							34
35							35
36							36

PROBLEM 4-1 ___ , Continued

5. *Omit "00" in the cents columns.*

Post-Closing Trial Balance

PROBLEM 4-2 ___

1.

Income Statement

Statement of Owner's Equity

Name _____

PROBLEM 4-2 _____, Continued

Balance Sheet

PROBLEM 4-3 ___

1.

Cash

Laundry Supplies

Prepaid Insurance

Laundry Equipment

Accumulated Depreciation

Accounts Payable

Wages Payable

_____,*Capital*

PROBLEM 4-3 ___, Continued

_____,Drawing

Income Summary

Laundry Revenue

Wages Expense

Rent Expense

Utilities Expense

Laundry Supplies Expense

Depreciation Expense

Insurance Expense

Miscellaneous Expense

PROBLEM 4-3 _____, Continued

2.

End-of-Period Spreadsheet (Work Sheet)

	A	B	C	D	E	F	G	H	I	J	K
	Account Title	Unadjusted Trial Balance		Adjustments		Adjusted Trial Balance		Income Statement		Balance Sheet	
		Dr.	Cr.	Dr.	Cr.	Dr.	Cr.	Dr.	Cr.	Dr.	Cr.
1											
2											
3											
4											
5											
6											
7											
8											
9											
10											
11											
12											
13											
14											
15											
16											
17											
18											
19											
20											
21											
22											

PROBLEM 4-3 ___, Continued

3.

		JOURNAL						PAGE		

	DATE		DESCRIPTION	POST. REF.	DEBIT	CREDIT	
1							1
2							2
3							3
4							4
5							5
6							6
7							7
8							8
9							9
10							10
11							11
12							12
13							13
14							14
15							15
16							16
17							17
18							18
19							19
20							20
21							21
22							22
23							23
24							24
25							25
26							26
27							27
28							28
29							29
30							30
31							31
32							32
33							33
34							34
35							35
36							36

PROBLEM 4-3 ___, Continued

4. *Omit "00" in the cents columns.*

Adjusted Trial Balances

PROBLEM 4-3 ___, Continued

5. *Omit "00" in the cents columns.*

Income Statement

Statement of Owner's Equity

PROBLEM 4-3 ___, Concluded

7. *Omit "00" in the cents columns.*

Post-Closing Trial Balance

Optional

1.

End-of-Period Spreadsheet (Work Sheet)

	A	B	C	D	E	F	G	H	I	J	K
	Account Title	Unadjusted Trial Balance		Adjustments		Adjusted Trial Balance		Income Statement		Balance Sheet	
		Dr.	Cr.	Dr.	Cr.	Dr.	Cr.	Dr.	Cr.	Dr.	Cr.
1	Cash	3,509									
2	Accounts Receivable	6,550									
3	Supplies	1,647									
4	Prepaid Insurance	1,800									
5	Land	30,000									
6	Building	57,500									
7	Accum. Depr.—Building		23,400								
8	Equipment	30,000									
9	Accum. Depr.—Equipment		10,200								
10	Accounts Payable		5,141								
11	Unearned Rent		2,200								
12	So Young Lee, Capital		67,825								
13	So Young Lee, Drawing	2,000									
14	Service Revenue		46,984								
15	Wages Expense	14,799									
16	Rent Expense	3,910									
17	Utilities Expense	1,728									
18	Miscellaneous Expense	2,307									
19		155,750	155,750								
20											
21											
22											

PROBLEM 4-4 ___, Continued

2.

	DATE		DESCRIPTION	POST. REF.	DEBIT	CREDIT	
1			*Adjusting Entries*				1
2							2
3							3
4							4
5							5
6							6
7							7
8							8
9							9
10							10
11							11
12							12
13							13
14							14
15							15
16							16
17							17
18							18
19							19
20							20
21							21
22							22
23							23
24							24
25							25
26							26
27							27
28							28
29							29
30							30
31							31
32							32
33							33
34							34
35							35
36							36

JOURNAL   PAGE

PROBLEM 4-4 ___ , Continued

3.

	Adjusted Trial Balance						

PROBLEM 4-4 ___, Continued

4.

Income Statement

Statement of Owner's Equity

PROBLEM 4-4 _____, Continued

Balance Sheet

PROBLEM 4-4 ___, Continued

5.

JOURNAL   PAGE 27

	DATE		DESCRIPTION	POST. REF.	DEBIT	CREDIT	
1			*Closing Entries*				1
2							2
3							3
4							4
5							5
6							6
7							7
8							8
9							9
10							10
11							11
12							12
13							13
14							14
15							15
16							16
17							17
18							18
19							19
20							20
21							21
22							22
23							23
24							24
25							25
26							26
27							27
28							28
29							29
30							30
31							31
32							32
33							33
34							34
35							35
36							36

PROBLEM 4-4 ___, Continued

6.

Post-Closing Trial Balance				

PROBLEM 4-4 ___ , Continued

2. and 5.

ACCOUNT   *Cash*   ACCOUNT NO.   *11*

DATE		ITEM	POST. REF.	DEBIT	CREDIT	BALANCE DEBIT	BALANCE CREDIT
2008 Mar.	1	Balance	√			1 2 5 9 00	
	3		23		9 1 0 00	3 4 9 00	
	4		23	5 0 0 0 00		5 3 4 9 00	
	5		23		8 6 00	5 2 6 3 00	
	7		23	8 0 0 00		6 0 6 3 00	
	8		23	4 0 0 00		6 4 6 3 00	
	8		23		2 5 8 4 00	3 8 7 9 00	
	8		23	1 6 9 5 00		5 5 7 4 00	
	10		24		5 1 0 00	5 0 6 4 00	
	12		24		2 3 1 9 00	2 7 4 5 00	
	15		24	2 7 1 8 00		5 4 6 3 00	
	16		24		1 0 0 0 00	4 4 6 3 00	
	19		24		2 1 3 5 00	2 3 2 8 00	
	22		24		3 7 0 00	1 9 5 8 00	
	22		24	3 9 9 2 00		5 9 5 0 00	
	24		25		5 2 7 00	5 4 2 3 00	
	26		25		2 4 8 0 00	2 9 4 3 00	
	30		25		1 5 6 00	2 7 8 7 00	
	30		25		2 6 00	2 7 6 1 00	
	31		25		1 0 0 0 00	1 7 6 1 00	
	31		25	2 0 2 9 00		3 7 9 0 00	
	31		25		2 8 1 00	3 5 0 9 00	

PROBLEM 4-4 ___, Continued

ACCOUNT   *Accounts Receivable*   ACCOUNT NO.   12

DATE		ITEM	POST. REF.	DEBIT	CREDIT	BALANCE DEBIT	BALANCE CREDIT
2008 Mar.	1	Balance	√			6 2 0 0 00	
	7		23		8 0 0 00	5 4 0 0 00	
	8		23		4 0 0 00	5 0 0 0 00	
	22		24	1 5 5 0 00		6 5 5 0 00	

ACCOUNT   *Supplies*   ACCOUNT NO.   13

DATE		ITEM	POST. REF.	DEBIT	CREDIT	BALANCE DEBIT	BALANCE CREDIT
2008 Mar.	1	Balance	√			6 1 0 00	
	10		24	5 1 0 00		1 1 2 0 00	
	27		25	5 2 7 00		1 6 4 7 00	

ACCOUNT   *Prepaid Insurance*   ACCOUNT NO.   14

DATE		ITEM	POST. REF.	DEBIT	CREDIT	BALANCE DEBIT	BALANCE CREDIT
2008 Mar.	1	Balance	√			4 2 0 00	
	22		24	1 3 8 0 00		1 8 0 0 00	

ACCOUNT   *Land*   ACCOUNT NO.   15

DATE		ITEM	POST. REF.	DEBIT	CREDIT	BALANCE DEBIT	BALANCE CREDIT
2008 Mar.	1	Balance	√			30 0 0 0 00	

PROBLEM 4-4 ___ , Continued

ACCOUNT   *Building*   ACCOUNT NO.   16

DATE		ITEM	POST. REF.	DEBIT	CREDIT	BALANCE DEBIT	BALANCE CREDIT
2008 Mar.	1	Balance	√			57 5 0 0 00	

ACCOUNT   *Accumulated Depreciation—Building*   ACCOUNT NO.   17

DATE		ITEM	POST. REF.	DEBIT	CREDIT	BALANCE DEBIT	BALANCE CREDIT
2008 Mar.	1	Balance	√				23 4 0 0 00

ACCOUNT   *Equipment*   ACCOUNT NO.   18

DATE		ITEM	POST. REF.	DEBIT	CREDIT	BALANCE DEBIT	BALANCE CREDIT
2008 Mar.	1	Balance	√			29 2 5 0 00	
	3		23	7 5 0 00		30 0 0 0 00	

ACCOUNT   *Accumulated Depreciation—Equipment*   ACCOUNT NO.   19

DATE		ITEM	POST. REF.	DEBIT	CREDIT	BALANCE DEBIT	BALANCE CREDIT
2008 Mar.	1	Balance	√				10 2 0 0 00

PROBLEM 4-4 ___, Continued

ACCOUNT   *Accounts Payable*   ACCOUNT NO.   21

DATE		ITEM	POST. REF.	DEBIT	CREDIT	BALANCE DEBIT	BALANCE CREDIT
2008 Mar.	1	Balance	√				8 6 2 5 00
	3		23		7 5 0 00		9 3 7 5 00
	8		23	2 5 8 4 00			6 7 9 1 00
	19		24	2 1 3 5 00			4 6 5 6 00
	31		25		4 8 5 00		5 1 4 1 00

ACCOUNT   *Wages Payable*   ACCOUNT NO.   22

DATE	ITEM	POST. REF.	DEBIT	CREDIT	BALANCE DEBIT	BALANCE CREDIT

ACCOUNT   *Unearned Rent*   ACCOUNT NO.   23

DATE		ITEM	POST. REF.	DEBIT	CREDIT	BALANCE DEBIT	BALANCE CREDIT
2008 Mar.	1	Balance	√				2 2 0 0 00

ACCOUNT   *So Young Lee, Capital*   ACCOUNT NO.   31

DATE		ITEM	POST. REF.	DEBIT	CREDIT	BALANCE DEBIT	BALANCE CREDIT
2008 Mar.	1	Balance	√				62 8 2 5 00
	4		23		5 0 0 0 00		67 8 2 5 00

PROBLEM 4-4 ___, Continued

ACCOUNT *So Young Lee, Drawing* ACCOUNT NO. **32**

DATE		ITEM	POST. REF.	DEBIT	CREDIT	BALANCE	
						DEBIT	CREDIT
2008 Mar.	16		24	1 0 0 0 00		1 0 0 0 00	
	31		25	1 0 0 0 00		2 0 0 0 00	

ACCOUNT *Income Summary* ACCOUNT NO. **33**

DATE	ITEM	POST. REF.	DEBIT	CREDIT	BALANCE	
					DEBIT	CREDIT

ACCOUNT *Service Revenue* ACCOUNT NO. **41**

DATE		ITEM	POST. REF.	DEBIT	CREDIT	BALANCE	
						DEBIT	CREDIT
2008 Mar.	8		23		9 6 9 5 00		14 6 9 5 00
	15		24		7 7 1 8 00		22 4 1 3 00
	22		24		8 9 9 2 00		31 4 0 5 00
	22		24		7 5 5 0 00		38 9 5 5 00
	31		25		8 0 2 9 00		46 9 8 4 00

PROBLEM 4-4 ___, Continued

ACCOUNT   *Rent Revenue*   ACCOUNT NO.   42

DATE	ITEM	POST. REF.	DEBIT	CREDIT	BALANCE DEBIT	BALANCE CREDIT

ACCOUNT   *Wages Expense*   ACCOUNT NO.   51

DATE		ITEM	POST. REF.	DEBIT	CREDIT	BALANCE DEBIT	BALANCE CREDIT
2008 Mar.	12		24	7 3 1 9 00		7 3 1 9 00	
	26		25	7 4 8 0 00		14 7 9 9 00	

ACCOUNT   *Supplies Expense*   ACCOUNT NO.   52

DATE	ITEM	POST. REF.	DEBIT	CREDIT	BALANCE DEBIT	BALANCE CREDIT

ACCOUNT   *Rent Expense*   ACCOUNT NO.   53

DATE		ITEM	POST. REF.	DEBIT	CREDIT	BALANCE DEBIT	BALANCE CREDIT
2008 Mar.	3		23	3 9 1 0 00		3 9 1 0 00	

PROBLEM 4-4 ___ , Continued

ACCOUNT *Depreciation Expense—Building*   ACCOUNT NO. 54

DATE		ITEM	POST. REF.	DEBIT	CREDIT	BALANCE DEBIT	BALANCE CREDIT

ACCOUNT *Utilities Expense*   ACCOUNT NO. 55

DATE		ITEM	POST. REF.	DEBIT	CREDIT	BALANCE DEBIT	BALANCE CREDIT
2008 Mar.	5		24	5 8 6 00		5 8 6 00	
	30		25	4 5 6 00		1 0 4 2 00	
	31		25	6 8 6 00		1 7 2 8 00	

ACCOUNT *Depreciation Expense—Equipment*   ACCOUNT NO. 56

DATE		ITEM	POST. REF.	DEBIT	CREDIT	BALANCE DEBIT	BALANCE CREDIT

ACCOUNT *Insurance Expense*   ACCOUNT NO. 57

DATE		ITEM	POST. REF.	DEBIT	CREDIT	BALANCE DEBIT	BALANCE CREDIT

PROBLEM 4-4 ____, Concluded

ACCOUNT   *Miscellaneous Expense*   ACCOUNT NO.   59

DATE		ITEM	POST. REF.	DEBIT	CREDIT	BALANCE DEBIT	BALANCE CREDIT
2008 Mar.	30		25	1 0 2 6 00		1 0 2 6 00	
	31		25	1 2 8 1 00		2 3 0 7 00	

This Page Not Used.

PROBLEM 4-5

2.

End-of-Period Spreadsheet (Work Sheet)

	A	B	C	D	E	F	G	H	I	J	K
	Account Title	Unadjusted Trial Balance		Adjustments		Adjusted Trial Balance		Income Statement		Balance Sheet	
		Dr.	Cr.	Dr.	Cr.	Dr.	Cr.	Dr.	Cr.	Dr.	Cr.
1											
2											
3											
4											
5											
6											
7											
8											
9											
10											
11											
12											
13											
14											
15											
16											
17											
18											
19											
20											
21											
22											
23											
24											
25											

PROBLEM 4-5 ___, Continued

3.

JOURNAL   PAGE

	DATE		DESCRIPTION	POST. REF.	DEBIT	CREDIT	
1			*Adjusting Entries*				1
2							2
3							3
4							4
5							5
6							6
7							7
8							8
9							9
10							10
11							11
12							12
13							13
14							14
15							15
16							16
17							17
18							18
19							19
20							20
21							21
22							22
23							23
24							24
25							25
26							26
27							27
28							28
29							29
30							30
31							31
32							32
33							33
34							34
35							35
36							36

PROBLEM 4-5 ___, Continued

4. *Omit "00" in the cents columns.*

Adjusted Trial Balance

PROBLEM 4-5 ___, Continued

5. *Omit "00" in the cents columns.*

Income Statement

Statement of Owner's Equity

Balance Sheet

PROBLEM 4-5 ___, Continued

1., 3., and 6.

ACCOUNT　*Cash*　　　　　　　　　ACCOUNT NO.　11

DATE	ITEM	POST. REF.	DEBIT	CREDIT	BALANCE	
					DEBIT	CREDIT

ACCOUNT　*Supplies*　　　　　　　　ACCOUNT NO.　13

DATE	ITEM	POST. REF.	DEBIT	CREDIT	BALANCE	
					DEBIT	CREDIT

ACCOUNT　*Prepaid Insurance*　　　　ACCOUNT NO.　14

DATE	ITEM	POST. REF.	DEBIT	CREDIT	BALANCE	
					DEBIT	CREDIT

ACCOUNT　*Equipment*　　　　　　　ACCOUNT NO.　16

DATE	ITEM	POST. REF.	DEBIT	CREDIT	BALANCE	
					DEBIT	CREDIT

ACCOUNT　*Accumulated Depreciation—Equipment*　　ACCOUNT NO.　17

DATE	ITEM	POST. REF.	DEBIT	CREDIT	BALANCE	
					DEBIT	CREDIT

PROBLEM 4-5 ____, Continued

ACCOUNT *Trucks* ACCOUNT NO. 18

DATE	ITEM	POST. REF.	DEBIT	CREDIT	BALANCE DEBIT	BALANCE CREDIT

ACCOUNT *Accumulated Depreciation—Trucks* ACCOUNT NO. 19

DATE	ITEM	POST. REF.	DEBIT	CREDIT	BALANCE DEBIT	BALANCE CREDIT

ACCOUNT *Accounts Payable* ACCOUNT NO. 21

DATE	ITEM	POST. REF.	DEBIT	CREDIT	BALANCE DEBIT	BALANCE CREDIT

ACCOUNT *Wages Payable* ACCOUNT NO. 22

DATE	ITEM	POST. REF.	DEBIT	CREDIT	BALANCE DEBIT	BALANCE CREDIT

ACCOUNT _____, *Capital* ACCOUNT NO. 31

DATE	ITEM	POST. REF.	DEBIT	CREDIT	BALANCE DEBIT	BALANCE CREDIT

ACCOUNT _____, *Drawing* ACCOUNT NO. 32

DATE	ITEM	POST. REF.	DEBIT	CREDIT	BALANCE DEBIT	BALANCE CREDIT

PROBLEM 4-5 ___, Continued

ACCOUNT   *Income Summary*   ACCOUNT NO.   33

DATE	ITEM	POST. REF.	DEBIT	CREDIT	BALANCE	
					DEBIT	CREDIT

ACCOUNT   *Service Revenue*   ACCOUNT NO.   41

DATE	ITEM	POST. REF.	DEBIT	CREDIT	BALANCE	
					DEBIT	CREDIT

ACCOUNT   *Wages Expense*   ACCOUNT NO.   51

DATE	ITEM	POST. REF.	DEBIT	CREDIT	BALANCE	
					DEBIT	CREDIT

ACCOUNT   *Supplies Expense*   ACCOUNT NO.   52

DATE	ITEM	POST. REF.	DEBIT	CREDIT	BALANCE	
					DEBIT	CREDIT

ACCOUNT   *Rent Expense*   ACCOUNT NO.   53

DATE	ITEM	POST. REF.	DEBIT	CREDIT	BALANCE	
					DEBIT	CREDIT

PROBLEM 4-5 ___, Continued

ACCOUNT   *Depreciation Expense—Equipment*   ACCOUNT NO.   54

DATE		ITEM	POST. REF.	DEBIT	CREDIT	BALANCE	
						DEBIT	CREDIT

ACCOUNT   *Truck Expense*   ACCOUNT NO.   55

DATE		ITEM	POST. REF.	DEBIT	CREDIT	BALANCE	
						DEBIT	CREDIT

ACCOUNT   *Depreciation Expense—Trucks*   ACCOUNT NO.   56

DATE		ITEM	POST. REF.	DEBIT	CREDIT	BALANCE	
						DEBIT	CREDIT

ACCOUNT   *Insurance Expense*   ACCOUNT NO.   57

DATE		ITEM	POST. REF.	DEBIT	CREDIT	BALANCE	
						DEBIT	CREDIT

ACCOUNT   *Miscellaneous Expense*   ACCOUNT NO.   59

DATE		ITEM	POST. REF.	DEBIT	CREDIT	BALANCE	
						DEBIT	CREDIT

PROBLEM 4-5 ___, Concluded

6.

JOURNAL

	DATE		DESCRIPTION	POST. REF.	DEBIT	CREDIT	
1			*Closing Entries*				1
2							2
3							3
4							4
5							5
6							6
7							7
8							8
9							9
10							10
11							11
12							12
13							13
14							14
15							15
16							16
17							17
18							18
19							19

7.

Post-Closing Trial Balance

PROBLEM 4-6 ___

1. and 2.   **JOURNAL**   PAGE 1

	DATE		DESCRIPTION	POST. REF.	DEBIT	CREDIT	
1							1
2							2
3							3
4							4
5							5
6							6
7							7
8							8
9							9
10							10
11							11
12							12
13							13
14							14
15							15
16							16
17							17
18							18
19							19
20							20
21							21
22							22
23							23
24							24
25							25
26							26
27							27
28							28
29							29
30							30
31							31
32							32
33							33
34							34
35							35
36							36

PROBLEM 4-6 ___ , Continued

JOURNAL   PAGE 2

	DATE		DESCRIPTION	POST. REF.	DEBIT	CREDIT	
1							1
2							2
3							3
4							4
5							5
6							6
7							7
8							8
9							9
10							10
11							11
12							12
13							13
14							14
15							15
16							16
17							17
18							18
19							19
20							20
21							21
22							22
23							23
24							24
25							25
26							26
27							27
28							28
29							29
30							30
31							31
32							32
33							33
34							34
35							35
36							36

PROBLEM 4-6 ___, Continued

2., 6., and 9.

ACCOUNT   *Cash*   ACCOUNT NO.   11

DATE	ITEM	POST. REF.	DEBIT	CREDIT	BALANCE DEBIT	BALANCE CREDIT
June 2008						

ACCOUNT   *Accounts Receivable*   ACCOUNT NO.   12

DATE	ITEM	POST. REF.	DEBIT	CREDIT	BALANCE DEBIT	BALANCE CREDIT
June 2008						

ACCOUNT   *Supplies*   ACCOUNT NO.   14

DATE	ITEM	POST. REF.	DEBIT	CREDIT	BALANCE DEBIT	BALANCE CREDIT
June 2008						

PROBLEM 4-6 ___, Continued

ACCOUNT   *Prepaid Rent*   ACCOUNT NO.   15

DATE	ITEM	POST. REF.	DEBIT	CREDIT	BALANCE DEBIT	BALANCE CREDIT
June 2008						

ACCOUNT   *Prepaid Insurance*   ACCOUNT NO.   16

DATE	ITEM	POST. REF.	DEBIT	CREDIT	BALANCE DEBIT	BALANCE CREDIT
June 2008						

ACCOUNT   *Office Equipment*   ACCOUNT NO.   18

DATE	ITEM	POST. REF.	DEBIT	CREDIT	BALANCE DEBIT	BALANCE CREDIT
June 2008						

ACCOUNT   *Accumulated Depreciation*   ACCOUNT NO.   19

DATE	ITEM	POST. REF.	DEBIT	CREDIT	BALANCE DEBIT	BALANCE CREDIT
June 2008						

ACCOUNT   *Accounts Payable*   ACCOUNT NO.   21

DATE	ITEM	POST. REF.	DEBIT	CREDIT	BALANCE DEBIT	BALANCE CREDIT
June 2008						

PROBLEM 4-6 ___, Continued

ACCOUNT   *Salaries Payable*   ACCOUNT NO.   *22*

DATE	ITEM	POST. REF.	DEBIT	CREDIT	BALANCE DEBIT	BALANCE CREDIT
June 2008						

ACCOUNT   *Unearned Fees*   ACCOUNT NO.   *23*

DATE	ITEM	POST. REF.	DEBIT	CREDIT	BALANCE DEBIT	BALANCE CREDIT
June 2008						

ACCOUNT   *, Capital*   ACCOUNT NO.   *31*

DATE	ITEM	POST. REF.	DEBIT	CREDIT	BALANCE DEBIT	BALANCE CREDIT
June 2008						

ACCOUNT   *, Drawing*   ACCOUNT NO.   *32*

DATE	ITEM	POST. REF.	DEBIT	CREDIT	BALANCE DEBIT	BALANCE CREDIT
June 2008						

ACCOUNT   *Income Summary*   ACCOUNT NO.   *33*

DATE	ITEM	POST. REF.	DEBIT	CREDIT	BALANCE DEBIT	BALANCE CREDIT
June 2008						

PROBLEM 4-6 ___ , Continued

ACCOUNT   *Fees Earned*   ACCOUNT NO.   41

DATE	ITEM	POST. REF.	DEBIT	CREDIT	BALANCE DEBIT	BALANCE CREDIT
June 2008						

ACCOUNT   *Salary Expense*   ACCOUNT NO.   51

DATE	ITEM	POST. REF.	DEBIT	CREDIT	BALANCE DEBIT	BALANCE CREDIT
June 2008						

ACCOUNT   *Rent Expense*   ACCOUNT NO.   52

DATE	ITEM	POST. REF.	DEBIT	CREDIT	BALANCE DEBIT	BALANCE CREDIT
June 2008						

ACCOUNT   *Supplies Expense*   ACCOUNT NO.   53

DATE	ITEM	POST. REF.	DEBIT	CREDIT	BALANCE DEBIT	BALANCE CREDIT
June 2008						

PROBLEM 4-6 ___ , Continued

ACCOUNT   *Depreciation Expense*   ACCOUNT NO.   54

DATE	ITEM	POST. REF.	DEBIT	CREDIT	BALANCE	
					DEBIT	CREDIT
June 2008						

ACCOUNT   *Insurance Expense*   ACCOUNT NO.   55

DATE	ITEM	POST. REF.	DEBIT	CREDIT	BALANCE	
					DEBIT	CREDIT
June 2008						

ACCOUNT   *Miscellaneous Expense*   ACCOUNT NO.   59

DATE	ITEM	POST. REF.	DEBIT	CREDIT	BALANCE	
					DEBIT	CREDIT
June 2008						

PROBLEM 4-6 ____, Continued

3.

Unadjusted Trial Balance		

PROBLEM 4-6 ___, Continued

6.

JOURNAL

	DATE		DESCRIPTION	POST. REF.	DEBIT	CREDIT	
1			*Adjusting Entries*				1
2							2
3							3
4							4
5							5
6							6
7							7
8							8
9							9
10							10
11							11
12							12
13							13
14							14
15							15
16							16
17							17
18							18
19							19
20							20
21							21
22							22
23							23
24							24
25							25
26							26
27							27
28							28
29							29
30							30
31							31
32							32
33							33
34							34
35							35
36							36

PROBLEM 4-6 ___ , Continued

7.

Adjusted Trial Balance									

PROBLEM 4-6 ___ , Continued

8.

Income Statement

Statement of Owner's Equity

Name _____

PROBLEM 4-6 ____, Continued

Balance Sheet

PROBLEM 4-6 _____, Continued

5. (optional)

End-of-Period Spreadsheet (Work Sheet)

	A	B	C	D	E	F	G	H	I	J	K
	Account Title	Unadjusted Trial Balance		Adjustments		Adjusted Trial Balance		Income Statement		Balance Sheet	
		Dr.	Cr.	Dr.	Cr.	Dr.	Cr.	Dr.	Cr.	Dr.	Cr.
1											
2											
3											
4											
5											
6											
7											
8											
9											
10											
11											
12											
13											
14											
15											
16											
17											
18											
19											
20											
21											
22											
23											
24											
25											

PROBLEM 4-6 ___, Concluded

9.

	DATE	DESCRIPTION	POST. REF.	DEBIT	CREDIT	
		JOURNAL			PAGE 3	
1		*Closing Entries*				1
2						2
3						3
4						4
5						5
6						6
7						7
8						8
9						9
10						10
11						11
12						12
13						13
14						14
15						15
16						16

10.

Post-Closing Trial Balance

CONTINUING PROBLEM

1.

End-of-Period Spreadsheet (Work Sheet)

	A	B	C	D	E	F	G	H	I	J	K
	Account Title	Unadjusted Trial Balance		Adjustments		Adjusted Trial Balance		Income Statement		Balance Sheet	
		Dr.	Cr.	Dr.	Cr.	Dr.	Cr.	Dr.	Cr.	Dr.	Cr.
1											
2											
3											
4											
5											
6											
7											
8											
9											
10											
11											
12											
13											
14											
15											
16											
17											
18											
19											
20											
21											
22											
23											
24											
25											

CONTINUING PROBLEM, Continued

2.

Income Statement

Statement of Owner's Equity

CONTINUING PROBLEM, Continued

3. Note: Use the general ledger accounts provided in Chapter 3, page 108.

	JOURNAL			PAGE 4

	DATE	DESCRIPTION	POST. REF.	DEBIT	CREDIT	
1		*Closing Entries*				1
2						2
3						3
4						4
5						5
6						6
7						7
8						8
9						9
10						10
11						11
12						12
13						13
14						14
15						15
16						16
17						17
18						18
19						19
20						20
21						21
22						22
23						23
24						24
25						25
26						26
27						27
28						28
29						29
30						30
31						31
32						32
33						33
34						34
35						35
36						36

204

Name

CONTINUING PROBLEM, Continued

Balance Sheet

CONTINUING PROBLEM, Concluded

4.

Post-Closing Trial Balance

This Page Not Used.

COMPREHENSIVE PROBLEM 1, Continued

1., 2., 6., and 9.

ACCOUNT   *Cash*   ACCOUNT NO.   *11*

DATE	ITEM	POST. REF.	DEBIT	CREDIT	BALANCE	
					DEBIT	CREDIT

ACCOUNT   *Accounts Receivable*   ACCOUNT NO.   *12*

DATE	ITEM	POST. REF.	DEBIT	CREDIT	BALANCE	
					DEBIT	CREDIT

ACCOUNT   *Supplies*   ACCOUNT NO.   *14*

DATE	ITEM	POST. REF.	DEBIT	CREDIT	BALANCE	
					DEBIT	CREDIT

COMPREHENSIVE PROBLEM 1, Continued

ACCOUNT *Prepaid Rent* ACCOUNT NO. 15

DATE	ITEM	POST. REF.	DEBIT	CREDIT	BALANCE	
					DEBIT	CREDIT

ACCOUNT *Prepaid Insurance* ACCOUNT NO. 16

DATE	ITEM	POST. REF.	DEBIT	CREDIT	BALANCE	
					DEBIT	CREDIT

ACCOUNT *Office Equipment* ACCOUNT NO. 18

DATE	ITEM	POST. REF.	DEBIT	CREDIT	BALANCE	
					DEBIT	CREDIT

ACCOUNT *Accumulated Depreciation* ACCOUNT NO. 19

DATE	ITEM	POST. REF.	DEBIT	CREDIT	BALANCE	
					DEBIT	CREDIT

ACCOUNT *Accounts Payable* ACCOUNT NO. 21

DATE	ITEM	POST. REF.	DEBIT	CREDIT	BALANCE	
					DEBIT	CREDIT

COMPREHENSIVE PROBLEM 1, Continued

ACCOUNT *Salaries Payable* ACCOUNT NO. 22

DATE	ITEM	POST. REF.	DEBIT	CREDIT	BALANCE DEBIT	BALANCE CREDIT

ACCOUNT *Unearned Fees* ACCOUNT NO. 23

DATE	ITEM	POST. REF.	DEBIT	CREDIT	BALANCE DEBIT	BALANCE CREDIT

ACCOUNT *Kelly Pitney, Capital* ACCOUNT NO. 31

DATE	ITEM	POST. REF.	DEBIT	CREDIT	BALANCE DEBIT	BALANCE CREDIT

ACCOUNT *Kelly Pitney, Drawing* ACCOUNT NO. 32

DATE	ITEM	POST. REF.	DEBIT	CREDIT	BALANCE DEBIT	BALANCE CREDIT

COMPREHENSIVE PROBLEM 1, Continued

ACCOUNT   *Income Summary*   ACCOUNT NO.   33

DATE	ITEM	POST. REF.	DEBIT	CREDIT	BALANCE	
					DEBIT	CREDIT

ACCOUNT   *Fees Earned*   ACCOUNT NO.   41

DATE	ITEM	POST. REF.	DEBIT	CREDIT	BALANCE	
					DEBIT	CREDIT

ACCOUNT   *Salary Expense*   ACCOUNT NO.   51

DATE	ITEM	POST. REF.	DEBIT	CREDIT	BALANCE	
					DEBIT	CREDIT

ACCOUNT   *Rent Expense*   ACCOUNT NO.   52

DATE	ITEM	POST. REF.	DEBIT	CREDIT	BALANCE	
					DEBIT	CREDIT

COMPREHENSIVE PROBLEM 1, Continued

ACCOUNT *Supplies Expense*   ACCOUNT NO. 53

DATE	ITEM	POST. REF.	DEBIT	CREDIT	BALANCE DEBIT	BALANCE CREDIT

ACCOUNT *Depreciation Expense*   ACCOUNT NO. 54

DATE	ITEM	POST. REF.	DEBIT	CREDIT	BALANCE DEBIT	BALANCE CREDIT

ACCOUNT *Insurance Expense*   ACCOUNT NO. 55

DATE	ITEM	POST. REF.	DEBIT	CREDIT	BALANCE DEBIT	BALANCE CREDIT

ACCOUNT *Miscellaneous Expense*   ACCOUNT NO. 59

DATE	ITEM	POST. REF.	DEBIT	CREDIT	BALANCE DEBIT	BALANCE CREDIT

COMPREHENSIVE PROBLEM 1, Continued

3.

	Unadjusted Trial Balance				

COMPREHENSIVE PROBLEM 1, Continued

5.

End-of-Period Spreadsheet (Work Sheet)

	A	B	C	D	E	F	G	H	I	J	K
	Account Title	Unadjusted Trial Balance		Adjustments		Adjusted Trial Balance		Income Statement		Balance Sheet	
		Dr.	Cr.	Dr.	Cr.	Dr.	Cr.	Dr.	Cr.	Dr.	Cr.
1											
2											
3											
4											
5											
6											
7											
8											
9											
10											
11											
12											
13											
14											
15											
16											
17											
18											
19											
20											
21											
22											
23											
24											
25											

COMPREHENSIVE PROBLEM 1, Continued

6.

JOURNAL   PAGE   7

	DATE		DESCRIPTION	POST. REF.	DEBIT	CREDIT	
1			*Adjusting Entries*				1
2							2
3							3
4							4
5							5
6							6
7							7
8							8
9							9
10							10
11							11
12							12
13							13
14							14
15							15
16							16
17							17
18							18
19							19
20							20
21							21
22							22
23							23
24							24
25							25
26							26
27							27
28							28
29							29
30							30
31							31
32							32
33							33
34							34
35							35
36							36

COMPREHENSIVE PROBLEM 1, Continued

7.

	Adjusted Trial Balance		

COMPREHENSIVE PROBLEM 1, Continued

8.

Income Statement

Statement of Owner's Equity

COMPREHENSIVE PROBLEM 1, Continued

Balance Sheet

Chapter 4

COMPREHENSIVE PROBLEM 1, Continued

9.

JOURNAL

PAGE 8

	DATE		DESCRIPTION	POST. REF.	DEBIT	CREDIT	
1			*Closing Entries*				1
2							2
3							3
4							4
5							5
6							6
7							7
8							8
9							9
10							10
11							11
12							12
13							13
14							14
15							15
16							16
17							17
18							18
19							19
20							20
21							21
22							22
23							23
24							24
25							25
26							26
27							27
28							28
29							29
30							30
31							31
32							32
33							33
34							34
35							35
36							36

COMPREHENSIVE PROBLEM 1, Concluded

10.

	Post-Closing Trial Balance		

This Page Not Used.

EXERCISE 5-1

REVENUE JOURNAL

Date	Invoice No.	Account Debited	Post. Ref.	Accounts Receivable Dr. Fees Earned Cr.
2008 Sept. 1	772	Environmental Safety Co.	(a) _____	$2,625
10	773	Greenberg Co.	(b) _____	1,050
20	774	Eco-Systems	(c) _____	1,400
27	775	SSC Corp.	(d) _____	965
30				$6,040
			(e) _____	

EXERCISE 5-2

a., b., and c.

GENERAL LEDGER

ACCOUNTS RECEIVABLE SUBSIDIARY LEDGER

EXERCISE 5-2 continued

d.

EXERCISE 5-3

a. _____

b. _____

c. _____

d. _____

e. _____

f. _____

g. _____

h. _____

i. _____

j. _____

EXERCISE 5-4

a. _____

b. _____

c. _____

d. _____

e. _____

f. _____

g. _____

h. _____

i. _____

j. _____

k. _____

EXERCISE 5-5

Dec. 3 _____

_____

_____

Dec. 9 _____

_____

_____

Dec. 13 _____

_____

_____

EXERCISE 5-6

a.

REVENUE JOURNAL   PAGE *8*

	DATE	INVOICE NO.	ACCOUNT DEBITED	POST. REF.	ACCTS. REC. DR. FEES EARNED CR.	
1						1
2						2
3						3
4						4
5						5
6						6
7						7
8						8
9						9
10						10
11						11
12						12
13						13
14						14
15						15

b. _____

_____

_____

c. _____

EXERCISE 5-7

a. and b.

Accounts Receivable—Ayres Co.

Accounts Receivable—Brown Co.

Accounts Receivable—Life Star Inc.

c.

Accounts Receivable—Control

Fees Earned

d.

Customer Balance Summary

EXERCISE 5-8

EXERCISE 5-9

REVENUE JOURNAL   PAGE 8

	DATE		INVOICE NO.	ACCOUNT DEBITED	POST. REF.	ACCTS. REC. DR. FEES EARNED CR.	
1							1
2							2
3							3
4							4
5							5
6							6
7							7
8							8
9							9
10							10
11							11
12							12
13							13
14							14
15							15

CASH RECEIPTS JOURNAL   PAGE 12

	DATE		ACCOUNT CREDITED	POST. REF.	FEES EARNED CR.	ACCOUNTS REC. CR.	CASH DR.	
1								1
2								2
3								3
4								4
5								5
6								6
7								7
8								8
9								9
10								10
11								11
12								12
13								13
14								14
15								15

EXERCISE 5-10

a.

REVENUE JOURNAL

PAGE *9*

	DATE		INVOICE NO.	ACCOUNT DEBITED	POST. REF.	ACCTS. REC. DR. FEES EARNED CR.	
1							1
2							2
3							3
4							4
5							5
6							6
7							7
8							8
9							9
10							10
11							11
12							12
13							13
14							14
15							15

CASH RECEIPTS JOURNAL

PAGE *25*

	DATE		ACCOUNT CREDITED	POST. REF.	FEES EARNED CR.	ACCOUNTS REC. CR.	CASH DR.	
1								1
2								2
3								3
4								4
5								5
6								6
7								7
8								8
9								9
10								10
11								11
12								12
13								13
14								14
15								15

EXERCISE 5-10 Concluded

b.

Customer Balance Summary

EXERCISE 5-11

a. _____

b. _____

c. _____

d. _____

e. _____

f. _____

g. _____

h. _____

i. _____

j. _____

k. _____

l. _____

m. _____

EXERCISE 5-12

a. _____

b. _____

c. _____

d. _____

e. _____

f. _____

g. _____

h. _____

i. _____

j. _____

k. _____

l. _____

EXERCISE 5-13

March 6   _____

_____

March 10   _____

_____

March 16   _____

_____

EXERCISE 5-14

PURCHASES JOURNAL

DATE	ACCOUNT CREDITED	POST. REF.	ACCOUNTS PAYABLE CR.	OFFICE SUPPLIES DR.	OTHER ACCOUNTS DR.			
					ACCOUNT	POST. REF.	AMOUNT	
1								1
2								2
3								3
4								4
5								5
6								6
7								7
8								8
9								9

b.

c.

EXERCISE 5-15
a. and b.

Accounts Payable—Best Cleaning Supplies Inc..

Accounts Payable—Lawson Co.

Accounts Payable—Office Mate Inc.

c.

Accounts Payable—Control

Cleaning Supplies

d.

Supplier Balance Summary

EXERCISE 5-16

EXERCISE 5-17

PURCHASES JOURNAL

PAGE 36

DATE	ACCOUNT CREDITED	POST. REF.	ACCOUNTS PAYABLE CR.	CLEANING SUPPLIES DR.	OTHER ACCOUNTS DR.		
					ACCOUNT	POST. REF.	AMOUNT
1							
2							
3							
4							
5							
6							
7							
8							
9							

CASH PAYMENTS JOURNAL

PAGE 41

DATE	CK. NO.	ACCOUNT DEBITED	POST. REF.	OTHER ACCOUNTS DR.	ACCOUNTS PAYABLE DR.	CASH CR.
1						
2						
3						
4						
5						
6						
7						
8						
9						

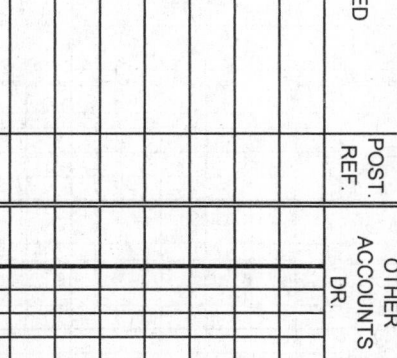

EXERCISE 5-18

a.

PURCHASES JOURNAL

PAGE 16

				ACCOUNTS PAYABLE CR.	PET SUPPLIES DR.	OTHER ACCOUNTS DR.		
DATE		ACCOUNT CREDITED	POST. REF.			ACCOUNT	POST. REF.	AMOUNT
1								
2								
3								
4								
5								
6								
7								
8								
9								

CASH PAYMENTS JOURNAL

PAGE 41

				OTHER ACCOUNTS DR.		ACCOUNTS PAYABLE DR.	CASH CR.
DATE	CK. NO.	ACCOUNT DEBITED	POST. REF.				
1							
2							
3							
4							
5							
6							
7							
8							
9							

EXERCISE 5-18, Concluded

b.

Supplier Balance Summary

EXERCISE 5-19

a.

EXERCISE 5-19, Continued

b.

Supplier Balance Summary Report

EXERCISE 5-20

Revenue journal: _____

Cash receipts journal: _____

Purchases journal: _____

Cash payments journal: _____

General journal: _____

EXERCISE 5-21

EXERCISE 5-22

a.

REVENUE JOURNAL

	DATE	INV. NO.	ACCOUNT DEBITED	POST. REF.	ACCOUNTS REC. DR.	FEES EARNED CR.	SALES TAX PAYABLE CR.	
1								1
2								2
3								3
4								4
5								5
6								6
7								7
8								8
9								9
10								10
11								11

JOURNAL

	DATE	DESCRIPTION	POST. REF.	DEBIT	CREDIT	
1						1
2						2
3						3
4						4
5						5
6						6
7						7

EXERCISE 5-22, Continued

ACCOUNTS RECEIVABLE SUBSIDIARY LEDGER

NAME

DATE	ITEM	POST. REF.	DEBIT	CREDIT	BALANCE

NAME

DATE	ITEM	POST. REF.	DEBIT	CREDIT	BALANCE

NAME

DATE	ITEM	POST. REF.	DEBIT	CREDIT	BALANCE

NAME

DATE	ITEM	POST. REF.	DEBIT	CREDIT	BALANCE

EXERCISE 5-22, Concluded

GENERAL LEDGER

b.

ACCOUNT *Accounts Receivable*   ACCOUNT NO. *12*

DATE	ITEM	POST. REF.	DEBIT	CREDIT	BALANCE	
					DEBIT	CREDIT

ACCOUNT *Office Supplies*   ACCOUNT NO. *14*

DATE	ITEM	POST. REF.	DEBIT	CREDIT	BALANCE	
					DEBIT	CREDIT

ACCOUNT *Sales Tax Payable*   ACCOUNT NO. *22*

DATE	ITEM	POST. REF.	DEBIT	CREDIT	BALANCE	
					DEBIT	CREDIT

ACCOUNT *Fees Earned*   ACCOUNT NO. *41*

DATE	ITEM	POST. REF.	DEBIT	CREDIT	BALANCE	
					DEBIT	CREDIT

c. 1. $ _____

2. $ _____

EXERCISE 5-23

a.–c.

EXERCISE 5-24

a.

Amazon.com

_____

_____

_____

_____

b.

Dell, Inc.

_____

_____

_____

_____

c.

W.S. Grainger, Inc.

_____

_____

_____

_____

d.

L.L. Bean, Inc.

_____

_____

_____

_____

e.

Smurfit-Stone Container Corporation

_____

_____

_____

_____

f.

Intuit, Inc.

_____

_____

_____

_____

This Page Not Used.

PROBLEM 5-1 ___

1. and 2.

REVENUE JOURNAL   PAGE 1

	DATE	INVOICE NO.	ACCOUNT DEBITED	POST. REF.	ACCTS. REC. DR. FEES EARNED CR.	
1						1
2						2
3						3
4						4
5						5
6						6
7						7
8						8
9						9
10						10
11						11

JOURNAL   PAGE 1

	DATE	DESCRIPTION	POST. REF.	DEBIT	CREDIT	
1						1
2						2
3						3
4						4
5						5
6						6

PROBLEM 5-1 ___, Continued

GENERAL LEDGER

2.

ACCOUNT _____   ACCOUNT NO. _____

DATE	ITEM	POST. REF.	DEBIT	CREDIT	BALANCE	
					DEBIT	CREDIT

ACCOUNT _____   ACCOUNT NO. _____

DATE	ITEM	POST. REF.	DEBIT	CREDIT	BALANCE	
					DEBIT	CREDIT

ACCOUNT _____   ACCOUNT NO. _____

DATE	ITEM	POST. REF.	DEBIT	CREDIT	BALANCE	
					DEBIT	CREDIT

ACCOUNTS RECEIVABLE LEDGER

1.

NAME _____

DATE	ITEM	POST. REF.	DEBIT	CREDIT	BALANCE

PROBLEM 5-1 ___, Continued

NAME

DATE	ITEM	POST. REF.	DEBIT	CREDIT	BALANCE

NAME

DATE	ITEM	POST. REF.	DEBIT	CREDIT	BALANCE

NAME

DATE	ITEM	POST. REF.	DEBIT	CREDIT	BALANCE

NAME

DATE	ITEM	POST. REF.	DEBIT	CREDIT	BALANCE

3. a. $ _____

   b. $ _____

4.

_____

_____

_____

PROBLEM 5-2 ___

GENERAL LEDGER

1. and 5.

ACCOUNT _____   ACCOUNT NO. _____

DATE	ITEM	POST. REF.	DEBIT	CREDIT	BALANCE	
					DEBIT	CREDIT

ACCOUNT _____   ACCOUNT NO. _____

DATE	ITEM	POST. REF.	DEBIT	CREDIT	BALANCE	
					DEBIT	CREDIT

ACCOUNT _____   ACCOUNT NO. _____

DATE	ITEM	POST. REF.	DEBIT	CREDIT	BALANCE	
					DEBIT	CREDIT

ACCOUNT _____   ACCOUNT NO. _____

DATE	ITEM	POST. REF.	DEBIT	CREDIT	BALANCE	
					DEBIT	CREDIT

6.

_____

_____

_____

PROBLEM 5-2 ___ , Continued

ACCOUNTS RECEIVABLE LEDGER

2. and 4.

NAME

DATE	ITEM	POST. REF.	DEBIT	CREDIT	BALANCE

NAME

DATE	ITEM	POST. REF.	DEBIT	CREDIT	BALANCE

NAME

DATE	ITEM	POST. REF.	DEBIT	CREDIT	BALANCE

NAME

DATE	ITEM	POST. REF.	DEBIT	CREDIT	BALANCE

PROBLEM 5-2 __, Continued

3., 4., and 5.

REVENUE JOURNAL   PAGE 40

	DATE	INVOICE NO.	ACCOUNT DEBITED	POST. REF.	ACCTS. REC. DR. FEES EARNED CR.	
1						1
2						2
3						3
4						4
5						5
6						6
7						7
8						8
9						9
10						10
11						11
12						12
13						13
14						14
15						15

JOURNAL   PAGE 1

	DATE	DESCRIPTION	POST. REF.	DEBIT	CREDIT	
1						1
2						2
3						3
4						4
5						5
6						6
7						7
8						8
9						9
10						10

PROBLEM 5-2 ___, Concluded

CASH RECEIPTS JOURNAL

	DATE	ACCOUNT CREDITED	POST. REF.	FEES EARNED CR.	ACCOUNTS REC. CR.	CASH DR.	
1							1
2							2
3							3
4							4
5							5
6							6
7							7
8							8
9							9
10							10
11							11
12							12
13							13
14							14
15							15
16							16
17							17
18							18
19							19
20							20
21							21
22							22
23							23
24							24
25							25
26							26
27							27
28							28
29							29
30							30
31							31
32							32
33							33
34							34
35							35

PROBLEM 5-3 ___

GENERAL LEDGER

1. and 4.

ACCOUNT   *Field Supplies*   ACCOUNT NO.   14

DATE	ITEM	POST. REF.	DEBIT	CREDIT	BALANCE	
					DEBIT	CREDIT

ACCOUNT   *Office Supplies*   ACCOUNT NO.   15

DATE	ITEM	POST. REF.	DEBIT	CREDIT	BALANCE	
					DEBIT	CREDIT

ACCOUNT   *Office Equipment*   ACCOUNT NO.   18

DATE	ITEM	POST. REF.	DEBIT	CREDIT	BALANCE	
					DEBIT	CREDIT

ACCOUNT   *Accounts Payable*   ACCOUNT NO.   21

DATE	ITEM	POST. REF.	DEBIT	CREDIT	BALANCE	
					DEBIT	CREDIT

PROBLEM 5-3 ___, Continued

ACCOUNTS PAYABLE SUBSIDIARY LEDGER

2. and 3.

NAME

DATE		ITEM	POST. REF.	DEBIT	CREDIT	BALANCE

NAME

DATE		ITEM	POST. REF.	DEBIT	CREDIT	BALANCE

NAME

DATE		ITEM	POST. REF.	DEBIT	CREDIT	BALANCE

NAME

DATE		ITEM	POST. REF.	DEBIT	CREDIT	BALANCE

NAME

DATE		ITEM	POST. REF.	DEBIT	CREDIT	BALANCE

5. a. $ _____

  b. $ _____

Name _____

PROBLEM 5-3 ____, Concluded

3. and 4.

PURCHASES JOURNAL

PAGE _30_

DATE	ACCOUNT CREDITED	POST. REF.	ACCOUNTS PAYABLE CR.	FIELD SUPPLIES DR.	OFFICE SUPPLIES DR.	OTHER ACCOUNTS DR.		
						ACCOUNT	POST. REF.	AMOUNT
1								
2								
3								
4								
5								
6								
7								
8								
9								
10								
11								
12								
13								
14								
15								
16								
17								
18								
19								
20								
21								
22								
23								

PROBLEM 5-4. ___

1., 2., and 3.

PURCHASES JOURNAL

PAGE 1

	DATE	ACCOUNT CREDITED	POST. REF.	ACCOUNTS PAYABLE CR.	FIELD SUPPLIES DR.	OFFICE SUPPLIES DR.	OTHER ACCOUNTS DR. ACCOUNT	POST. REF.	AMOUNT	
1										1
2										2
3										3
4										4
5										5
6										6
7										7
8										8
9										9
10										10
11										11
12										12
13										13
14										14
15										15
16										16
17										17
18										18
19										19
20										20
21										21
22										22
23										23

PROBLEM 5-4 ___, Continued

1., 2., and 3.   CASH PAYMENTS JOURNAL   PAGE 1

	DATE	CK. NO.	ACCOUNT DEBITED	POST. REF.	OTHER ACCOUNTS DR.	ACCOUNTS PAYABLE DR.	CASH CR.	
1								1
2								2
3								3
4								4
5								5
6								6
7								7
8								8
9								9
10								10
11								11
12								12
13								13
14								14
15								15
16								16
17								17

1. and 2.   JOURNAL   PAGE 1

	DATE	DESCRIPTION	POST. REF.	DEBIT	CREDIT	
1						1
2						2
3						3
4						4
5						5
6						6
7						7
8						8
9						9
10						10
11						11
12						12

PROBLEM 5-4 ___ , Continued

ACCOUNTS PAYABLE LEDGER

1.

NAME

DATE		ITEM	POST. REF.	DEBIT	CREDIT	BALANCE

NAME

DATE		ITEM	POST. REF.	DEBIT	CREDIT	BALANCE

NAME

DATE		ITEM	POST. REF.	DEBIT	CREDIT	BALANCE

PROBLEM 5-4 ___, Continued

GENERAL LEDGER

2. and 3.

ACCOUNT _____   ACCOUNT NO. _____

DATE	ITEM	POST. REF.	DEBIT	CREDIT	BALANCE DEBIT	BALANCE CREDIT

ACCOUNT _____   ACCOUNT NO. _____

DATE	ITEM	POST. REF.	DEBIT	CREDIT	BALANCE DEBIT	BALANCE CREDIT

ACCOUNT _____   ACCOUNT NO. _____

DATE	ITEM	POST. REF.	DEBIT	CREDIT	BALANCE DEBIT	BALANCE CREDIT

ACCOUNT _____   ACCOUNT NO. _____

DATE	ITEM	POST. REF.	DEBIT	CREDIT	BALANCE DEBIT	BALANCE CREDIT

ACCOUNT _____   ACCOUNT NO. _____

DATE	ITEM	POST. REF.	DEBIT	CREDIT	BALANCE DEBIT	BALANCE CREDIT

PROBLEM 5-4 ____, Continued

ACCOUNT   ACCOUNT NO.

DATE	ITEM	POST. REF.	DEBIT	CREDIT	BALANCE	
					DEBIT	CREDIT

ACCOUNT   ACCOUNT NO.

DATE	ITEM	POST. REF.	DEBIT	CREDIT	BALANCE	
					DEBIT	CREDIT

ACCOUNT   ACCOUNT NO.

DATE	ITEM	POST. REF.	DEBIT	CREDIT	BALANCE	
					DEBIT	CREDIT

ACCOUNT   ACCOUNT NO.

DATE	ITEM	POST. REF.	DEBIT	CREDIT	BALANCE	
					DEBIT	CREDIT

ACCOUNT   ACCOUNT NO.

DATE	ITEM	POST. REF.	DEBIT	CREDIT	BALANCE	
					DEBIT	CREDIT

PROBLEM 5-4 ___ , Concluded

4.

Supplier Balance Summary				

EXERCISE 6-1

a. _____

b. _____

c. _____

_____

_____

EXERCISE 6-2

_____

EXERCISE 6-3

a. Purchases − (X + Y) = Net purchases

_____

b. Net purchases + X = Cost of merchandise purchased

_____

c. Merchandise inventory (beginning) + Cost of merchandise purchased = X

_____

d. Merchandise available for sale − X = Cost of merchandise sold

_____

EXERCISE 6-4

a.

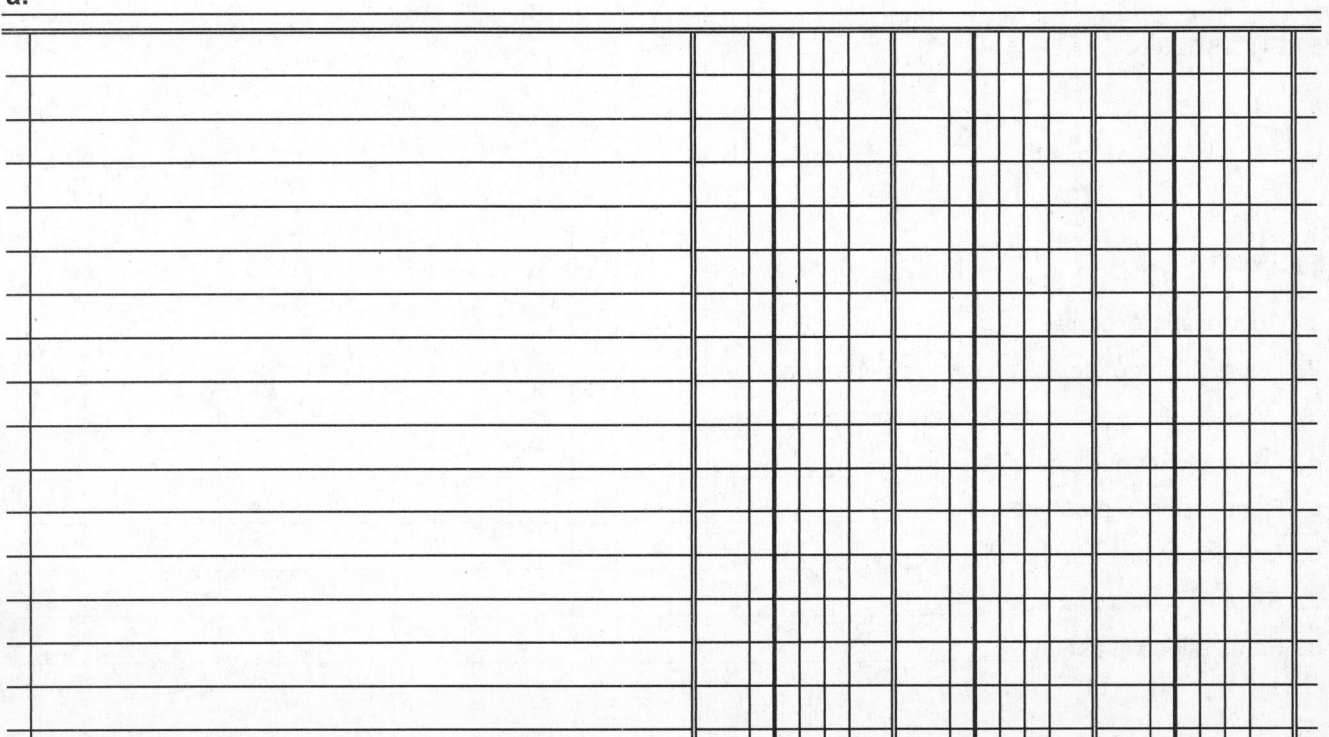

EXERCISE 6-4, Concluded

b. _____

EXERCISE 6-5

_____
_____
_____
_____
_____
_____
_____
_____
_____
_____
_____
_____
_____
_____
_____
_____
_____

EXERCISE 6-6

a. Net Sales: _____

b. Gross Profit: _____

EXERCISE 6-7

1. Advertising expense: _____

2. Depreciation expense on store equipment: _____

3. Insurance expense on office equipment: _____

4. Interest expense on notes payable: _____

5. Rent expense on office building: _____

6. Salaries of office personnel: _____

7. Salary of sales manager: _____

8. Sales supplies used: _____

EXERCISE 6-8

EXERCISE 6-9

EXERCISE 6-10

a. _____

b. _____

c. _____

d. _____

e. _____

f. _____

g. _____

h. _____

EXERCISE 6-11

a.

_____

_____

b.

_____

_____

_____

_____

_____

EXERCISE 6-12

Balance Sheet Accounts		Income Statement Accounts	
Acct #	**Account Name**	**Acct #**	**Account Name**

EXERCISE 6-13

JOURNAL   PAGE

	DATE		DESCRIPTION	POST. REF.	DEBIT	CREDIT	
1							1
2							2
3							3
4							4
5							5
6							6
7							7
8							8
9							9
10							10
11							11
12							12
13							13
14							14
15							15
16							16
17							17
18							18
19							19
20							20
21							21
22							22
23							23
24							24
25							25
26							26
27							27
28							28
29							29
30							30
31							31
32							32
33							33
34							34
35							35
36							36

EXERCISE 6-14

_____

_____

_____

_____

_____

_____

_____

_____

_____

_____

EXERCISE 6-15

a. _____

_____

b.

JOURNAL

PAGE

	DATE		DESCRIPTION	POST. REF.	DEBIT	CREDIT	
1							1
2							2
3							3
4							4
5							5
6							6

EXERCISE 6-16

(1) _____

_____

(2) _____

_____

(3) _____

_____

(4) _____

_____

(5) _____

_____

EXERCISE 6-17

a. Amount of the sale: _____

b. Amount debited to Accounts Receivable: _____

c. Amount of the discount for early payment: _____

d. Amount due within the discount period: _____

EXERCISE 6-18

a. _____

b. _____

EXERCISE 6-19

_____

_____

_____

_____

_____

_____

_____

_____

_____

EXERCISE 6-20

(1) _____

_____

(2) _____

_____

_____

(3) _____

_____

(4) _____

_____

_____

EXERCISE 6-21

a.–c.

JOURNAL   PAGE _____

	DATE		DESCRIPTION	POST. REF.	DEBIT	CREDIT	
1							1
2							2
3							3
4							4
5							5
6							6
7							7
8							8
9							9
10							10

EXERCISE 6-22

JOURNAL   PAGE _____

	DATE		DESCRIPTION	POST. REF.	DEBIT	CREDIT	
1							1
2							2
3							3
4							4
5							5
6							6
7							7
8							8
9							9
10							10
11							11
12							12
13							13
14							14
15							15
16							16

EXERCISE 6-23

	Merchandise	Transportation Paid by Seller		Returns and Allowances	Amount to be Paid in Full
a.	$8,000	—	FOB shipping point, 1/10, n/30	$1,500	$ _____
b.	2,900	$125	FOB shipping point, 2/10, n/30	400	$ _____
c.	3,850	—	FOB destination, 2/10, n/30	—	$ _____
d.	15,000	—	FOB destination, n/30	2,500	$ _____
e.	5,000	275	FOB shipping point, 2/10, n/30	1,000	$ _____

EXERCISE 6-24

a. _____

b. _____

c. _____

d. _____

EXERCISE 6-25

a. and b.

JOURNAL   PAGE

	DATE		DESCRIPTION	POST. REF.	DEBIT	CREDIT	
1							1
2							2
3							3
4							4
5							5
6							6
7							7
8							8
9							9
10							10
11							11
12							12

EXERCISE 6-26

a.–c.

JOURNAL

	DATE	DESCRIPTION	POST. REF.	DEBIT	CREDIT	
1						1
2						2
3						3
4						4
5						5
6						6
7						7
8						8
9						9
10						10
11						11
12						12
13						13
14						14
15						15
16						16
17						17
18						18

EXERCISE 6-27

a.–c.

JOURNAL

	DATE	DESCRIPTION	POST. REF.	DEBIT	CREDIT	
1						1
2						2
3						3
4						4
5						5
6						6
7						7
8						8
9						9
10						10
11						11
12						12

EXERCISE 6-28

		Debit	Credit
a.	Sales..	_____	_____
b.	Sales Discounts...........................	_____	_____
c.	Sales Returns and Allowances	_____	_____
d.	Cost of Merchandise Sold	_____	_____
e.	Delivery Expense	_____	_____
f.	Merchandise Inventory............................	_____	_____
g.	Sales Tax Payable	_____	_____

EXERCISE 6-29

JOURNAL   PAGE ____

	DATE	DESCRIPTION	POST. REF.	DEBIT	CREDIT	
1						1
2						2
3						3

EXERCISE 6-30

(a) Accounts Payable: _____

(b) Advertising Expenses: _____

(c) Cost of Merchandise sold: _____

(d) Merchandise Inventory: _____

(e) Sales: _____

(f) Sales Discounts: _____

(g) Sales Returns and Allowances: _____

(h) Supplies: _____

(i) Supplies Expense: _____

(j) Terry Weaver, Drawing: _____

(k) Wages Payable: _____

EXERCISE 6-31

JOURNAL

	DATE		DESCRIPTION	POST. REF.	DEBIT	CREDIT	
1							1
2							2
3							3
4							4
5							5
6							6
7							7
8							8
9							9
10							10
11							11
12							12
13							13
14							14
15							15
16							16
17							17
18							18
19							19
20							20
21							21
22							22
23							23

EXERCISE 6-32

JOURNAL   PAGE

	DATE		DESCRIPTION	POST. REF.	DEBIT	CREDIT	
1							1
2							2
3							3
4							4
5							5
6							6
7							7
8							8
9							9
10							10
11							11
12							12
13							13
14							14
15							15
16							16
17							17

EXERCISE 6-33

a. 2005: _____

2004: _____

b. _____

_____

_____

_____

_____

_____

_____

_____

EXERCISE 6-34

a. _____

b. _____

_____

_____

_____

_____

_____

_____

_____

_____

_____

Name _____

Chapter 6

APPENDIX 1—EXERCISE 6-35

a. and c.

SALES JOURNAL

PAGE ____

DATE	INVOICE NO.	ACCOUNT DEBITED	POST. REF.	ACCOUNTS RECEIVABLE DR. SALES CR.	COST OF MERCHANDISE SOLD DR. MERCHANDISE INVENTORY CR.	
						1
						2
						3
						4
						5
						6
						7
						8

b. and c.

PURCHASES JOURNAL

PAGE ____

DATE	ACCOUNT CREDITED	POST. REF.	ACCOUNTS PAYABLE CR.	MERCHANDISE INVENTORY DR.	OTHER ACCOUNTS DR.	POST. REF.	AMOUNT	
								1
								2
								3
								4
								5
								6
								7
								8

APPENDIX 1—EXERCISE 6-35, Concluded

d.

_____

_____

_____

_____

_____

_____

_____

_____

_____

APPENDIX 2—EXERCISE 6-36

1. _____
2. _____
3. _____
4. _____
5. _____
6. _____
7. _____
8. _____
9. _____
10. _____

APPENDIX 2—EXERCISE 6-37

a. _____

b. _____

c. _____

d. _____

e. _____

f. _____

g. _____

APPENDIX 2—EXERCISE 6-38

JOURNAL

PAGE _____

	DATE		DESCRIPTION	POST. REF.	DEBIT	CREDIT	
1							1
2							2
3							3
4							4
5							5
6							6
7							7
8							8
9							9
10							10
11							11
12							12
13							13
14							14
15							15
16							16
17							17
18							18
19							19
20							20
21							21
22							22

APPENDIX 2—EXERCISE 6-39

JOURNAL

	DATE		DESCRIPTION	POST. REF.	DEBIT	CREDIT	
1							1
2							2
3							3
4							4
5							5
6							6
7							7
8							8
9							9
10							10
11							11
12							12
13							13
14							14
15							15
16							16
17							17
18							18
19							19
20							20
21							21
22							22
23							23
24							24
25							25

APPENDIX 2—EXERCISE 6-40

JOURNAL

	DATE		DESCRIPTION	POST. REF.	DEBIT	CREDIT	
1							1
2							2
3							3
4							4
5							5
6							6
7							7
8							8
9							9
10							10
11							11
12							12
13							13
14							14
15							15
16							16
17							17
18							18
19							19
20							20
21							21
22							22
23							23
24							24
25							25

PROBLEM 6-1 ___

1. *Omit "00" in the cents columns.*

Income Statement

PROBLEM 6-1 ___ , Continued

2. *Omit "00" in the cents columns.*

Statement of Owner's Equity

PROBLEM 6-1 ___, Continued

3. *Omit "00" in the cents columns.*

	Balance Sheet														

PROBLEM 6-1 ___ , Concluded

4. a. _____

_____

_____

_____

_____

_____

_____

_____

_____

_____

_____

_____

_____

_____

_____

_____

b. _____

_____

_____

_____

_____

_____

_____

_____

_____

_____

_____

_____

_____

_____

_____

_____

_____

_____

PROBLEM 6-2 ___

1. *Omit "00" in the cents columns.*

Income Statement

2. *Omit "00" in the cents columns.*

Statement of Owner's Equity

Name _____

PROBLEM 6-2 _____ , Continued

3. *Omit "00" in the cents columns.*

Balance Sheet

PROBLEM 6-2 ___, Concluded

4.

JOURNAL

	DATE		DESCRIPTION	POST. REF.	DEBIT	CREDIT	
1							1
2							2
3							3
4							4
5							5
6							6
7							7
8							8
9							9
10							10
11							11
12							12
13							13
14							14
15							15
16							16
17							17
18							18
19							19
20							20
21							21
22							22
23							23
24							24
25							25
26							26
27							27
28							28
29							29
30							30
31							31
32							32
33							33
34							34
35							35
36							36

Page not used.

PROBLEM 6-3 ___

JOURNAL   PAGE

	DATE	DESCRIPTION	POST. REF.	DEBIT	CREDIT	
1						1
2						2
3						3
4						4
5						5
6						6
7						7
8						8
9						9
10						10
11						11
12						12
13						13
14						14
15						15
16						16
17						17
18						18
19						19
20						20
21						21
22						22
23						23
24						24
25						25
26						26
27						27
28						28
29						29
30						30
31						31
32						32
33						33
34						34
35						35
36						36

PROBLEM 6-3 ____, Concluded

JOURNAL   PAGE

	DATE		DESCRIPTION	POST. REF.	DEBIT	CREDIT	
1							1
2							2
3							3
4							4
5							5
6							6
7							7
8							8
9							9
10							10
11							11
12							12
13							13
14							14
15							15
16							16
17							17
18							18
19							19
20							20
21							21
22							22
23							23
24							24
25							25
26							26
27							27
28							28
29							29
30							30
31							31
32							32
33							33
34							34
35							35
36							36

PROBLEM 6-4 ___

JOURNAL

	DATE		DESCRIPTION	POST. REF.	DEBIT	CREDIT	
1							1
2							2
3							3
4							4
5							5
6							6
7							7
8							8
9							9
10							10
11							11
12							12
13							13
14							14
15							15
16							16
17							17
18							18
19							19
20							20
21							21
22							22
23							23
24							24
25							25
26							26
27							27
28							28
29							29
30							30
31							31
32							32
33							33
34							34
35							35
36							36

PROBLEM 6- 4___, Concluded

JOURNAL   PAGE

	DATE	DESCRIPTION	POST. REF.	DEBIT	CREDIT	
1						1
2						2
3						3
4						4
5						5
6						6
7						7
8						8
9						9
10						10
11						11
12						12
13						13
14						14
15						15
16						16
17						17
18						18
19						19
20						20
21						21
22						22
23						23
24						24
25						25
26						26
27						27
28						28
29						29
30						30
31						31
32						32
33						33
34						34
35						35
36						36

PROBLEM 6-5 ___

JOURNAL   PAGE ___

	DATE		DESCRIPTION	POST. REF.	DEBIT	CREDIT	
1							1
2							2
3							3
4							4
5							5
6							6
7							7
8							8
9							9
10							10
11							11
12							12
13							13
14							14
15							15
16							16
17							17
18							18
19							19
20							20
21							21
22							22
23							23
24							24
25							25
26							26
27							27
28							28
29							29
30							30
31							31
32							32
33							33
34							34
35							35
36							36

PROBLEM 6-5___ , Concluded

JOURNAL   PAGE

	DATE		DESCRIPTION	POST. REF.	DEBIT	CREDIT	
1							1
2							2
3							3
4							4
5							5
6							6
7							7
8							8
9							9
10							10
11							11
12							12
13							13
14							14
15							15
16							16
17							17
18							18
19							19
20							20
21							21
22							22
23							23
24							24
25							25
26							26
27							27
28							28
29							29
30							30
31							31
32							32
33							33
34							34
35							35
36							36

PROBLEM 6-7 ___

JOURNAL

	DATE		DESCRIPTION	POST. REF.	DEBIT	CREDIT	
1							1
2							2
3							3
4							4
5							5
6							6
7							7
8							8
9							9
10							10
11							11
12							12
13							13
14							14
15							15
16							16
17							17
18							18
19							19
20							20
21							21
22							22
23							23
24							24
25							25
26							26
27							27
28							28
29							29
30							30
31							31
32							32
33							33
34							34
35							35
36							36

This Page Not Used.

PROBLEM 6-8 ___

JOURNAL

	DATE		DESCRIPTION	POST. REF.	DEBIT	CREDIT	
1							1
2							2
3							3
4							4
5							5
6							6
7							7
8							8
9							9
10							10
11							11
12							12
13							13
14							14
15							15
16							16
17							17
18							18
19							19
20							20
21							21
22							22
23							23
24							24
25							25
26							26
27							27
28							28
29							29
30							30
31							31
32							32
33							33
34							34
35							35
36							36

This Page Not Used.

PROBLEM 6-10 ___

1.

_____

_____

_____

2.

_____

Income Statement

PROBLEM 6-10 ___, Continued

2.

Income Statement (Continued)

PROBLEM 6-10 ____, Concluded

3.

JOURNAL

	DATE		DESCRIPTION	POST. REF.	DEBIT	CREDIT	
1							1
2							2
3							3
4							4
5							5
6							6
7							7
8							8
9							9
10							10
11							11
12							12
13							13
14							14
15							15
16							16
17							17
18							18
19							19
20							20
21							21
22							22
23							23
24							24
25							25
26							26
27							27
28							28
29							29
30							30
31							31
32							32
33							33
34							34
35							35

This Page Not Used.

COMPREHENSIVE PROBLEM 2

1., 2., 6., and 9.

ACCOUNT   *Cash*   ACCOUNT NO. *110*

DATE	ITEM	POST. REF.	DEBIT	CREDIT	BALANCE DEBIT	BALANCE CREDIT

COMPREHENSIVE PROBLEM 2, Continued

ACCOUNT   *Accounts Receivable*   ACCOUNT NO. *112*

DATE	ITEM	POST. REF.	DEBIT	CREDIT	BALANCE DEBIT	BALANCE CREDIT

ACCOUNT   *Merchandise Inventory*   ACCOUNT NO. *115*

DATE	ITEM	POST. REF.	DEBIT	CREDIT	BALANCE DEBIT	BALANCE CREDIT

COMPREHENSIVE PROBLEM 2, Continued

ACCOUNT   *Prepaid Insurance*   ACCOUNT NO.   116

DATE		ITEM	POST. REF.	DEBIT	CREDIT	BALANCE	
						DEBIT	CREDIT

ACCOUNT   *Store Supplies*   ACCOUNT NO.   117

DATE		ITEM	POST. REF.	DEBIT	CREDIT	BALANCE	
						DEBIT	CREDIT

ACCOUNT   *Store Equipment*   ACCOUNT NO.   123

DATE		ITEM	POST. REF.	DEBIT	CREDIT	BALANCE	
						DEBIT	CREDIT

ACCOUNT   *Accumulated Depreciation—Store Equipment*   ACCOUNT NO.   124

DATE		ITEM	POST. REF.	DEBIT	CREDIT	BALANCE	
						DEBIT	CREDIT

COMPREHENSIVE PROBLEM 2, Continued

ACCOUNT   *Accounts Payable*   ACCOUNT NO.   *210*

DATE	ITEM	POST. REF.	DEBIT	CREDIT	BALANCE DEBIT	BALANCE CREDIT

ACCOUNT   *Salaries Payable*   ACCOUNT NO.   *211*

DATE	ITEM	POST. REF.	DEBIT	CREDIT	BALANCE DEBIT	BALANCE CREDIT

ACCOUNT   *Evan Raskind, Capital*   ACCOUNT NO.   *310*

DATE	ITEM	POST. REF.	DEBIT	CREDIT	BALANCE DEBIT	BALANCE CREDIT

ACCOUNT   *Evan Raskind, Drawing*   ACCOUNT NO.   *311*

DATE	ITEM	POST. REF.	DEBIT	CREDIT	BALANCE DEBIT	BALANCE CREDIT

COMPREHENSIVE PROBLEM 2, Continued

ACCOUNT   *Income Summary*   ACCOUNT NO.   *312*

DATE	ITEM	POST. REF.	DEBIT	CREDIT	BALANCE DEBIT	BALANCE CREDIT

ACCOUNT   *Sales*   ACCOUNT NO.   *410*

DATE	ITEM	POST. REF.	DEBIT	CREDIT	BALANCE DEBIT	BALANCE CREDIT

ACCOUNT   *Sales Returns and Allowances*   ACCOUNT NO.   *411*

DATE	ITEM	POST. REF.	DEBIT	CREDIT	BALANCE DEBIT	BALANCE CREDIT

COMPREHENSIVE PROBLEM 2, Continued

ACCOUNT   *Sales Discounts*   ACCOUNT NO.   412

DATE	ITEM	POST. REF.	DEBIT	CREDIT	BALANCE DEBIT	BALANCE CREDIT

ACCOUNT   *Cost of Merchandise Sold*   ACCOUNT NO.   510

DATE	ITEM	POST. REF.	DEBIT	CREDIT	BALANCE DEBIT	BALANCE CREDIT

ACCOUNT   *Sales Salaries Expense*   ACCOUNT NO.   520

DATE	ITEM	POST. REF.	DEBIT	CREDIT	BALANCE DEBIT	BALANCE CREDIT

COMPREHENSIVE PROBLEM 2, Continued

ACCOUNT *Advertising Expense* ACCOUNT NO. *521*

DATE	ITEM	POST. REF.	DEBIT	CREDIT	BALANCE DEBIT	BALANCE CREDIT

ACCOUNT *Depreciation Expense* ACCOUNT NO. *522*

DATE	ITEM	POST. REF.	DEBIT	CREDIT	BALANCE DEBIT	BALANCE CREDIT

ACCOUNT *Store Supplies Expense* ACCOUNT NO. *523*

DATE	ITEM	POST. REF.	DEBIT	CREDIT	BALANCE DEBIT	BALANCE CREDIT

ACCOUNT *Miscellaneous Selling Expense* ACCOUNT NO. *529*

DATE	ITEM	POST. REF.	DEBIT	CREDIT	BALANCE DEBIT	BALANCE CREDIT

COMPREHENSIVE PROBLEM 2, Continued

ACCOUNT *Office Salaries Expense*   ACCOUNT NO. 530

DATE	ITEM	POST. REF.	DEBIT	CREDIT	BALANCE	
					DEBIT	CREDIT

ACCOUNT *Rent Expense*   ACCOUNT NO. 531

DATE	ITEM	POST. REF.	DEBIT	CREDIT	BALANCE	
					DEBIT	CREDIT

ACCOUNT *Insurance Expense*   ACCOUNT NO. 532

DATE	ITEM	POST. REF.	DEBIT	CREDIT	BALANCE	
					DEBIT	CREDIT

ACCOUNT *Miscellaneous Administrative Expense*   ACCOUNT NO. 539

DATE	ITEM	POST. REF.	DEBIT	CREDIT	BALANCE	
					DEBIT	CREDIT

COMPREHENSIVE PROBLEM 2, Continued
1. and 2.

JOURNAL   PAGE *20*

	DATE		DESCRIPTION	POST. REF.	DEBIT	CREDIT	
1							1
2							2
3							3
4							4
5							5
6							6
7							7
8							8
9							9
10							10
11							11
12							12
13							13
14							14
15							15
16							16
17							17
18							18
19							19
20							20
21							21
22							22
23							23
24							24
25							25
26							26
27							27
28							28
29							29
30							30
31							31
32							32
33							33
34							34
35							35
36							36

COMPREHENSIVE PROBLEM 2, Continued

JOURNAL

PAGE *20*
continued

	DATE		DESCRIPTION	POST. REF.	DEBIT	CREDIT	
1							1
2							2
3							3
4							4
5							5
6							6
7							7
8							8
9							9
10							10
11							11
12							12
13							13
14							14
15							15

JOURNAL

PAGE *21*

	DATE		DESCRIPTION	POST. REF.	DEBIT	CREDIT	
1							1
2							2
3							3
4							4
5							5
6							6
7							7
8							8
9							9
10							10
11							11
12							12
13							13
14							14
15							15
16							16

COMPREHENSIVE PROBLEM 2, Continued

JOURNAL

	DATE		DESCRIPTION	POST. REF.	DEBIT	CREDIT	
1							1
2							2
3							3
4							4
5							5
6							6
7							7
8							8
9							9
10							10
11							11
12							12
13							13
14							14
15							15
16							16
17							17
18							18
19							19
20							20
21							21
22							22
23							23
24							24
25							25
26							26
27							27
28							28
29							29
30							30
31							31
32							32
33							33
34							34
35							35
36							36

COMPREHENSIVE PROBLEM 2, Continued

3.

Unadjusted Trial Balance		

COMPREHENSIVE PROBLEM 2, Continued

4. and 6.

JOURNAL

	DATE		DESCRIPTION	POST. REF.	DEBIT	CREDIT	
1			*Adjusting Entries*				1
2							2
3							3
4							4
5							5
6							6
7							7
8							8
9							9
10							10
11							11
12							12
13							13
14							14
15							15
16							16
17							17
18							18
19							19
20							20
21							21
22							22
23							23
24							24
25							25
26							26
27							27
28							28
29							29
30							30
31							31
32							32
33							33
34							34
35							35
36							36

COMPREHENSIVE PROBLEM 2, Continued

7.

	Adjusted Trial Balance		

COMPREHENSIVE PROBLEM 2, Continued

8. *Omit "00" in the cents columns.*

Income Statement

COMPREHENSIVE PROBLEM 2, Continued

Omit "00" in the cents columns.

Statement of Owner's Equity								

COMPREHENSIVE PROBLEM 2, Continued

Omit "00" in the cents columns.

Balance Sheet

COMPREHENSIVE PROBLEM 2, Continued

9.

JOURNAL   PAGE *3*

	DATE		DESCRIPTION	POST. REF.	DEBIT	CREDIT	
1			*Closing Entries*				1
2							2
3							3
4							4
5							5
6							6
7							7
8							8
9							9
10							10
11							11
12							12
13							13
14							14
15							15
16							16
17							17
18							18
19							19
20							20
21							21
22							22
23							23
24							24
25							25
26							26
27							27
28							28
29							29
30							30
31							31
32							32
33							33
34							34
35							35
36							36

COMPREHENSIVE PROBLEM 2, Concluded

10. *Omit "00" in the cents columns.*

Post-Closing Trial Balance

336

COMPREHENSIVE PROBLEM 2, Concluded

alt. 5. *This work sheet is applicable only if following alternative instructions.*

End-of-Period Spreadsheet (Work Sheet)

Account Title	Unadjusted Trial Balance Dr.	Cr.	Adjustments Dr.	Cr.	Adjusted Trial Balance Dr.	Cr.	Income Statement Dr.	Cr.	Balance Sheet Dr.	Cr.	
											1
											2
											3
											4
											5
											6
											7
											8
											9
											10
											11
											12
											13
											14
											15
											16
											17
											18
											19
											20
											21
											22
											23
											24
											25
											26

EXERCISE 7-1

_____

_____

_____

_____

_____

_____

_____

_____

_____

_____

_____

_____

_____

EXERCISE 7-2

a. _____

_____

_____

_____

b. _____

_____

_____

_____

c. _____

_____

_____

_____

EXERCISE 7-3

Portable MP3 Players

Date	Purchases			Cost of Merchandise Sold			Inventory		
	Quantity	Unit Cost	Total Cost	Quantity	Unit Cost	Total Cost	Quantity	Unit Cost	Total Cost

Portable MP3 Players

Date	Purchases			Cost of Merchandise Sold			Inventory		
	Quantity	Unit Cost	Total Cost	Quantity	Unit Cost	Total Cost	Quantity	Unit Cost	Total Cost

EXERCISE 7-5

Cell Phones

Date	Purchases			Cost of Merchandise Sold			Inventory		
	Quantity	Unit Cost	Total Cost	Quantity	Unit Cost	Total Cost	Quantity	Unit Cost	Total Cost

EXERCISE 7-6

Cell Phones

Date	Purchases			Cost of Merchandise Sold			Inventory		
	Quantity	Unit Cost	Total Cost	Quantity	Unit Cost	Total Cost	Quantity	Unit Cost	Total Cost

EXERCISE 7-7

a. FIFO: _____

b. LIFO: _____

EXERCISE 7-8

a. First-in, first-out method: _____

_____

b. Last-in, first-out method: _____

_____

c. Average cost method: _____

_____

_____

_____

_____

_____

_____

EXERCISE 7-9

Inventory Method	Cost	
	Merchandise Inventory	**Merchandise Sold**
a. First-in, first-out................	_____	_____
b. Last-in, first-out................	_____	_____
c. Average cost...................	_____	_____

Supporting calculations:

_____

_____

_____

_____

_____

_____

_____

_____

_____

_____

_____

_____

_____

EXERCISE 7-10

a. FIFO inventory _____ LIFO inventory

b. FIFO cost of goods sold _____ LIFO cost of goods sold

c. FIFO net income _____ LIFO net income

d. FIFO income tax _____ LIFO income tax

2. _____

_____

_____

_____

_____

_____

_____

_____

_____

_____

_____

_____

_____

_____

_____

_____

_____

_____

_____

_____

EXERCISE 7-11

Commodity	Inventory Quantity	Unit Cost Price	Unit Market Price	Total		
				Cost	Market	Lower of C or M
62CF3	10	$120	$131	$	$	$
41DH2	35	80	75			
03MQ3	10	275	260			
23FH6	16	40	28			
10KT4	40	90	94			
Total				$	$	$

EXERCISE 7-12

_____

_____

_____

_____

_____

EXERCISE 7-13

a.   **Balance Sheet**

Merchandise inventory ....   _____

Current assets ....   _____

Total assets ....   _____

Owner's equity ....   _____

b.   **Income Statement**

Cost of merchandise sold ....   _____

Gross profit ....   _____

Net income...   _____

EXERCISE 7-14

a.   **Balance Sheet**

Merchandise inventory ....   _____

Current assets ....   _____

Total assets ....   _____

Owner's equity ....   _____

b.   **Income Statement**

Cost of merchandise sold ....   _____

Gross profit ....   _____

Net income...   _____

EXERCISE 7-15

EXERCISE 7-16

EXERCISE 7-17

	COST	RETAIL

EXERCISE 7-18

a.

b. _____

_____

_____

_____

_____

EXERCISE 7-19

a. Apple Computer: _____

_____

American Greetings: _____

_____

b. _____

_____

_____

_____

_____

_____

_____

_____

EXERCISE 7-20

a. Number of Days' Sales in Inventory:

_____

Albertson's _____

_____

_____

Kroger _____

_____

_____

Safeway _____

_____

_____

Inventory Turnover:

_____

Albertson's _____

_____

_____

Kroger _____

_____

_____

Safeway _____

_____

_____

b. _____

_____

_____

_____

_____

_____

EXERCISE 7-20, Concluded

c.

PROBLEM 7-4 ___

Inventory Sheet

December 31, 2008

Description	Inventory Quantity	Unit Cost Price	Unit Market Price	Total Cost	Total Market	Lower of C or M
AC172	~~35~~ 25	$60	$ 56	$1,500	$1,400	
	13	58		754	728	
				2,254	2,128	$2,128
BE43	18		180			
CJ9	30		120			
E34	125		26			
F17	18		550			
G68	60		15			
K41	5		390			
Q79	375		6			
RZ13	90		18			
S60	6		235			
W21	140		18			
XR90	15		745			

Page not used.

PROBLEM 7-5 ___

1. *Omit "00" in the cents columns.*

	COST	RETAIL

PROBLEM 7-5 ___ , Concluded

2. **a.** *Omit "00" in the cents columns.*

b. *Omit "00" in the cents columns.*

EXERCISE 8-1

EXERCISE 8-2

a. _____

b. _____

c. _____

EXERCISE 8-3

a. _____

b. _____

c. _____

d. _____

EXERCISE 8-4

EXERCISE 8-5

EXERCISE 8-6

EXERCISE 8-7

EXERCISE 8-8

a. _____

b. _____

EXERCISE 8-9

a. _____

_____

_____

_____

_____

_____

_____

b. _____

_____

_____

_____

_____

_____

_____

EXERCISE 8-10

EXERCISE 8-11

a.

b.

EXERCISE 8-12

JOURNAL   PAGE

	DATE	DESCRIPTION	POST. REF.	DEBIT	CREDIT	
1						1
2						2
3						3
4						4
5						5
6						6
7						7
8						8
9						9
10						10
11						11
12						12
13						13
14						14

EXERCISE 8-13

JOURNAL   PAGE

	DATE	DESCRIPTION	POST. REF.	DEBIT	CREDIT	
1						1
2						2
3						3
4						4
5						5
6						6
7						7
8						8
9						9
10						10
11						11
12						12
13						13
14						14

EXERCISE 8-14

EXERCISE 8-15

_____
_____
_____
_____
_____
_____
_____
_____
_____
_____
_____
_____
_____
_____
_____
_____
_____
_____
_____
_____
_____

EXERCISE 8-16

a. Addition to the balance per bank: _____

b. Deduction from the balance per bank: _____

c. Addition to the balance per company records: _____

d. Deduction from the balance per company's records: _____

EXERCISE 8-17

_____

EXERCISE 8-18

EXERCISE 8-19

JOURNAL

PAGE

	DATE		DESCRIPTION	POST. REF.	DEBIT	CREDIT	
1							1
2							2
3							3
4							4
5							5

EXERCISE 8-20

JOURNAL

PAGE

	DATE		DESCRIPTION	POST. REF.	DEBIT	CREDIT	
1							1
2							2
3							3
4							4

EXERCISE 8-21

a.

b. _____

EXERCISE 8-22

EXERCISE 8-22, Concluded

EXERCISE 8-23

a. _____

b.

EXERCISE 8-24

a. and b.

JOURNAL PAGE

	DATE		DESCRIPTION	POST. REF.	DEBIT	CREDIT	
1							1
2							2
3							3
4							4
5							5
6							6
7							7
8							8

EXERCISE 8-25

EXERCISE 8-26

a.

b.

EXERCISE   8-27

Part (a)

_____

_____

Part (b)

_____

_____

Part (c)

_____

_____

_____

_____

_____

_____

_____

_____

_____

_____

_____

_____

Exercise   8-28

Part (a)

_____

_____

Part (b)

_____

_____

Part (c)

_____

_____

_____

_____

_____

_____

This Page Not Used.

PROBLEM 8-1 ___

This Page Not Used.

PROBLEM 8-2 ___

JOURNAL   PAGE

	DATE		DESCRIPTION	POST. REF.	DEBIT	CREDIT	
1							1
2							2
3							3
4							4
5							5
6							6
7							7
8							8
9							9
10							10
11							11
12							12
13							13
14							14
15							15
16							16
17							17
18							18
19							19
20							20
21							21
22							22
23							23
24							24
25							25
26							26
27							27
28							28
29							29
30							30
31							31
32							32
33							33
34							34
35							35
36							36

This Page Not Used.

PROBLEM 8-3 ___

1.

_____
_____
_____

		DEBIT		CREDIT	

2.

JOURNAL   PAGE ___

	DATE	DESCRIPTION	POST. REF.	DEBIT	CREDIT	
1						1
2						2
3						3
4						4
5						5
6						6
7						7

This Page Not Used.

PROBLEM 8-4 ___

1.

PROBLEM 8-4 ___, Concluded

2.

	DATE		DESCRIPTION	POST. REF.	DEBIT	CREDIT	
1							1
2							2
3							3
4							4
5							5
6							6
7							7
8							8
9							9
10							10
11							11
12							12
13							13
14							14
15							15
16							16
17							17
18							18
19							19
20							20
21							21
22							22
23							23
24							24
25							25
26							26
27							27
28							28
29							29
30							30
31							31
32							32
33							33
34							34
35							35
36							36

JOURNAL   PAGE

PROBLEM 8-5 ___

1.

PROBLEM 8-5 ____, Concluded

2.

JOURNAL   PAGE

	DATE		DESCRIPTION	POST. REF.	DEBIT	CREDIT	
1							1
2							2
3							3
4							4
5							5
6							6
7							7
8							8
9							9
10							10
11							11
12							12
13							13
14							14
15							15
16							16
17							17
18							18
19							19
20							20
21							21
22							22
23							23
24							24

3. $ _____

4.

_____

_____

_____

_____

_____

_____

EXERCISE 9-1

_____
_____
_____
_____
_____
_____
_____

EXERCISE 9-2

a. _____
_____
_____

b. _____
_____
_____

c. _____
_____
_____
_____
_____
_____
_____
_____

EXERCISE 9-3

JOURNAL

PAGE

	DATE		DESCRIPTION	POST. REF.	DEBIT	CREDIT	
1							1
2							2
3							3
4							4
5							5
6							6
7							7
8							8
9							9
10							10
11							11
12							12
13							13
14							14
15							15
16							16
17							17
18							18
19							19
20							20

EXERCISE 9-4

<table>
<tr><td align="center" colspan="6">**JOURNAL**</td><td align="center">PAGE</td></tr>
<tr><td colspan="2">DATE</td><td>DESCRIPTION</td><td>POST. REF.</td><td>DEBIT</td><td>CREDIT</td><td></td></tr>
<tr><td></td><td></td><td></td><td></td><td></td><td></td><td>1</td></tr>
<tr><td></td><td></td><td></td><td></td><td></td><td></td><td>2</td></tr>
<tr><td></td><td></td><td></td><td></td><td></td><td></td><td>3</td></tr>
<tr><td></td><td></td><td></td><td></td><td></td><td></td><td>4</td></tr>
<tr><td></td><td></td><td></td><td></td><td></td><td></td><td>5</td></tr>
<tr><td></td><td></td><td></td><td></td><td></td><td></td><td>6</td></tr>
<tr><td></td><td></td><td></td><td></td><td></td><td></td><td>7</td></tr>
<tr><td></td><td></td><td></td><td></td><td></td><td></td><td>8</td></tr>
<tr><td></td><td></td><td></td><td></td><td></td><td></td><td>9</td></tr>
<tr><td></td><td></td><td></td><td></td><td></td><td></td><td>10</td></tr>
<tr><td></td><td></td><td></td><td></td><td></td><td></td><td>11</td></tr>
<tr><td></td><td></td><td></td><td></td><td></td><td></td><td>12</td></tr>
<tr><td></td><td></td><td></td><td></td><td></td><td></td><td>13</td></tr>
<tr><td></td><td></td><td></td><td></td><td></td><td></td><td>14</td></tr>
<tr><td></td><td></td><td></td><td></td><td></td><td></td><td>15</td></tr>
<tr><td></td><td></td><td></td><td></td><td></td><td></td><td>16</td></tr>
<tr><td></td><td></td><td></td><td></td><td></td><td></td><td>17</td></tr>
</table>

EXERCISE 9-5

a.–b.

<table>
<tr><td align="center" colspan="6">**JOURNAL**</td><td align="center">PAGE</td></tr>
<tr><td colspan="2">DATE</td><td>DESCRIPTION</td><td>POST. REF.</td><td>DEBIT</td><td>CREDIT</td><td></td></tr>
<tr><td></td><td></td><td></td><td></td><td></td><td></td><td>1</td></tr>
<tr><td></td><td></td><td></td><td></td><td></td><td></td><td>2</td></tr>
<tr><td></td><td></td><td></td><td></td><td></td><td></td><td>3</td></tr>
<tr><td></td><td></td><td></td><td></td><td></td><td></td><td>4</td></tr>
<tr><td></td><td></td><td></td><td></td><td></td><td></td><td>5</td></tr>
<tr><td></td><td></td><td></td><td></td><td></td><td></td><td>6</td></tr>
<tr><td></td><td></td><td></td><td></td><td></td><td></td><td>7</td></tr>
<tr><td></td><td></td><td></td><td></td><td></td><td></td><td>8</td></tr>
<tr><td></td><td></td><td></td><td></td><td></td><td></td><td>9</td></tr>
<tr><td></td><td></td><td></td><td></td><td></td><td></td><td>10</td></tr>
</table>

EXERCISE 9-6

a. _____

b. _____

c. _____

b. _____

EXERCISE 9-7

Account	Due Date	Number of Days Past Due
Ben's Pickup Shop	June 9	
Bumper Auto	July 10	
Downtown Repair	March 18	
Jake's Auto Repair	May 19	
Like New	June 18	
Sally's	April 12	
Uptown Auto	May 8	
Yellowstone Repair & Tow	April 15	

EXERCISE 9-8

a.

Customer	Due Date	Number of Days Past Due
Tamika Industries	August 24	
Ruppert Company	September 3	
Weborne Inc.	October 17	
Kristi Company	November 5	
Simrill Company	December 3	

EXERCISE 9-8, Concluded

b.

Aging-of-Receivables Schedule
November 30

CUSTOMER	BALANCE	NOT PAST DUE	DAYS PAST DUE 1–30	31–60	61–90	OVER 90
Aaron Brothers Inc.	2 0 0 0 0 0	2 0 0 0 0 0				
Abell Company	1 5 0 0 0		1 5 0 0 0			
~						
Zollo Company	5 0 0 0 0 0			5 0 0 0 0 0		
Subtotals	7 7 2 5 0 0 0 0	4 4 0 0 0 0 0 0	1 8 0 0 0 0 0 0	7 8 5 0 0 0 0	4 2 3 0 0 0 0	3 1 7 0 0 0 0

EXERCISE 9-9

BALANCE	NOT PAST DUE	DAYS PAST DUE 1–30	31–60	61–90	OVER 90

EXERCISE 9-10

JOURNAL   PAGE

	DATE		DESCRIPTION	POST. REF.	DEBIT	CREDIT	
1							1
2							2
3							3
4							4
5							5

EXERCISE 9-11

Age Interval	Balance	Estimated Uncollectible Accounts	
		Percent	**Amount**
Not past due.............................	$400,000	1%	$ _____
1–30 days past due............................	80,000	2	_____
31–60 days past due	18,000	5	_____
61–90 days past due..........................	12,500	10	_____
91–180 days past due.........................	6,000	70	_____
Over 180 days past due......................	2,500	90	_____
Total..	$519,000		$ _____

EXERCISE 9-12

JOURNAL   PAGE

	DATE		DESCRIPTION	POST. REF.	DEBIT	CREDIT	
1							1
2							2
3							3
4							4
5							5

EXERCISE 9-13

a.

JOURNAL PAGE

	DATE	DESCRIPTION	POST. REF.	DEBIT	CREDIT	
1						1
2						2
3						3
4						4
5						5
6						6
7						7
8						8
9						9
10						10
11						11
12						12
13						13
14						14
15						15
16						16
17						17
18						18
19						19
20						20
21						21
22						22
23						23
24						24
25						25
26						26
27						27
28						28
29						29
30						30
31						31
32						32
33						33
34						34
35						35
36						36

EXERCISE 9-13, Concluded

b.

JOURNAL

	DATE	DESCRIPTION	POST. REF.	DEBIT	CREDIT	
1						1
2						2
3						3
4						4
5						5
6						6
7						7
8						8
9						9
10						10
11						11
12						12
13						13
14						14
15						15
16						16
17						17
18						18
19						19
20						20
21						21
22						22
23						23
24						24

c.

EXERCISE 9-14

a.

	DATE		DESCRIPTION	POST. REF.	DEBIT	CREDIT	
1							1
2							2
3							3
4							4
5							5
6							6
7							7
8							8
9							9
10							10
11							11
12							12
13							13
14							14
15							15
16							16
17							17
18							18
19							19
20							20
21							21
22							22
23							23
24							24
25							25
26							26
27							27
28							28
29							29
30							30
31							31
32							32
33							33
34							34
35							35
36							36

EXERCISE 9-14 Continued

b.

Aging Class	Receivables Balance on Dec. 31	Estimated Percent of Uncollectible Accounts	Computations
1–30 days past due............................	160,000	3%	
31–60 days past due	40,000	10	
61–90 days past due...........................	18,000	20	
91–120 days past due.........................	11,000	40	
More than 120 days past due	6,500	75	
Total Receivables...........................	$519,000		

c.

EXERCISE 9-15

EXERCISE 9-16

a. _____

b. _____

EXERCISE 9-17

a.

JOURNAL

PAGE

	DATE		DESCRIPTION	POST. REF.	DEBIT	CREDIT	
1							1
2							2
3							3
4							4
5							5
6							6

b.

JOURNAL

PAGE

	DATE		DESCRIPTION	POST. REF.	DEBIT	CREDIT	
1							1
2							2
3							3
4							4
5							5
6							6
7							7
8							8
9							9
10							10

c. _____

_____

_____

_____

EXERCISE   9-18

a.

	DATE	DESCRIPTION	POST. REF.	DEBIT	CREDIT	
1						1
2						2
3						3
4						4
5						5
6						6

JOURNAL   PAGE

b.

JOURNAL   PAGE

	DATE	DESCRIPTION	POST. REF.	DEBIT	CREDIT	
1						1
2						2
3						3
4						4
5						5
6						6
7						7
8						8
9						9
10						10

Aging Class	Receivables Balance on Dec. 31	Estimated Percent of Uncollectible Accounts	Computations
1–30 days past due............................	380,000	2%	_____
31–60 days past due	70,000	5	_____
61–90 days past due..........................	30,000	15	_____
91–120 days past due........................	25,000	25	_____
More than 120 days past due	10,000	50	_____
Total Receivables..........................	$515,000		

EXERCISE 9-19

	Date of Note	Face Amount	Term of Note	Interest Rate	Due Date	Interest Due
a.	May 5	$ 15,000	60 days	9%	_____	$ _____
b.	July 19	8,000	60 days	10%	_____	_____
c.	August 31	5,000	90 days	12%	_____	_____
d.	Dec. 28	18,000	120 days	10%	_____	_____
e.	Nov. 30	10,500	60 days	12%	_____	_____

EXERCISE 9-20

a. _____

b. _____

c. (1) and (2)

JOURNAL   PAGE

	DATE		DESCRIPTION	POST. REF.	DEBIT	CREDIT	
1							1
2							2
3							3
4							4
5							5
6							6

EXERCISE 9-21

1. _____

2. _____

3. _____

4. _____

5. _____

6. _____

7. _____

EXERCISE 9-22

JOURNAL

	DATE	DESCRIPTION	POST. REF.	DEBIT	CREDIT	
1						1
2						2
3						3
4						4
5						5
6						6
7						7
8						8
9						9
10						10
11						11
12						12
13						13
14						14
15						15

EXERCISE 9-23

JOURNAL

PAGE

	DATE	DESCRIPTION	POST. REF.	DEBIT	CREDIT	
1						1
2						2
3						3
4						4
5						5
6						6
7						7
8						8
9						9
10						10
11						11

EXERCISE 9-24

	DATE		DESCRIPTION	POST. REF.	DEBIT	CREDIT	
1							1
2							2
3							3
4							4
5							5
6							6
7							7
8							8
9							9
10							10
11							11
12							12
13							13
14							14
15							15
16							16
17							17
18							18
19							19
20							20
21							21

JOURNAL   PAGE

EXERCISE 9-25

_____

_____

_____

_____

_____

_____

EXERCISE 9-26

a. and b.   **2005**   **2004**

Net Sales_____

Accounts Receivable_____

Average Accounts Receivable_____

Accounts Receivable turnover_____

Average Daily Sales _____

Days' Sales in Receivables _____

c _____

   _____

   _____

   _____

EXERCISE 9-27

a. 2005: _____

   2004: _____

b. 2005 : _____

   2004: _____

c. _____

   _____

   _____

EXERCISE 9-28

a. and b.   **2005**   **2004**

Net Sales_____

Accounts Receivable_____

Average Accounts Receivable_____

Accounts Receivable turnover_____

Average Daily Sales _____

Days' Sales in Receivables _____

c _____

   _____

   _____

   _____

EXERCISE 9-29

a. The Limited, Inc. _____

_____

H.J. Heinz Company: _____

_____

b. _____

c. _____

_____

_____

_____

_____

_____

_____

_____

_____

_____

APPENDIX EXERCISE 9-30

a. _____

b. _____

c. _____

d. _____

e.

JOURNAL

PAGE

	DATE		DESCRIPTION	POST. REF.	DEBIT	CREDIT	
1							1
2							2
3							3
4							4

APPENDIX EXERCISE 9-31

JOURNAL   PAGE _____

	DATE		DESCRIPTION	POST. REF.	DEBIT	CREDIT	
1							1
2							2
3							3
4							4
5							5
6							6
7							7
8							8
9							9
10							10
11							11
12							12
13							13
14							14
15							15
16							16
17							17
18							18
19							19
20							20
21							21
22							22

PROBLEM   9-2 ___

1.

Customer	Due Date	Number of Days Past Due

4.

JOURNAL   PAGE

	DATE		DESCRIPTION	POST. REF.	DEBIT	CREDIT	
1							1
2							2
3							3
4							4
5							5
6							6
7							7
8							8
9							9
10							10
11							11
12							12
13							13
14							14
15							15

PROBLEM 9-2 _____, Concluded

2. and 3.

Aging-of-Receivables Schedule

December 31, 2006

CUSTOMER	BALANCE	NOT PAST DUE	1–30	31–60	DAYS PAST DUE 61–90	91–120	OVER 120

PROBLEM   9-3 ___

Year	Bad Debt Expense			Balance of Allowance Account, End of Year
	Expense Actually Reported	Expense Based on Estimate	Increase (Decrease) in Amount of Expense	

2.

This Page Not Used.

PROBLEM   9-5 ___

JOURNAL

	DATE		DESCRIPTION	POST. REF.	DEBIT	CREDIT	
1							1
2							2
3							3
4							4
5							5
6							6
7							7
8							8
9							9
10							10
11							11
12							12
13							13
14							14
15							15
16							16
17							17
18							18
19							19
20							20
21							21
22							22
23							23
24							24
25							25
26							26
27							27
28							28
29							29
30							30
31							31
32							32
33							33
34							34
35							35
36							36

416

This Page Not Used.

EXERCISE 10-1

a. New printing press costs debited to the asset account:

_____

_____

_____

_____

b. Secondhand printing press costs debited to the asset account:

_____

_____

_____

_____

EXERCISE 10-2

a. _____

_____

_____

b. _____

_____

_____

EXERCISE 10-3

EXERCISE 10-4

1. _____
2. _____
3. _____
4. _____
5. _____
6. _____
7. _____
8. _____
9. _____
10. _____

EXERCISE 10-5

1. _____
2. _____
3. _____
4. _____
5. _____
6. _____
7. _____
8. _____
9. _____
10. _____

EXERCISE 10-6

JOURNAL   PAGE

	DATE	DESCRIPTION	POST. REF.	DEBIT	CREDIT	
1						1
2						2
3						3
4						4
5						5
6						6
7						7
8						8

EXERCISE 10-7

a. _____

_____

_____

_____

b. _____

_____

_____

_____

EXERCISE 10-8

a. 2 years: _____

b. 8 years: _____

c. 10 years: _____

d. 20 years: _____

e. 25 years: _____

f. 40 years: _____

g. 50 years: _____

EXERCISE 10-9

_____

_____

EXERCISE 10-10

_____

_____

_____

_____

EXERCISE 10-11

a.

Truck No.	Rate per Mile	Miles Operated	Credit to Accumulated Depreciation
1	_____	_____	$_____
2	_____	_____	$_____
3	_____	_____	$_____
4	_____	_____	$_____
Total			$_____

b.

JOURNAL   PAGE

	DATE		DESCRIPTION	POST. REF.	DEBIT	CREDIT	
1							1
2							2
3							3

EXERCISE 10-12

a. Straight-line method:

First year: _____

Second year: _____

b. Double-declining-balance method:

First year: _____

Second year: _____

EXERCISE 10-13

a. Straight-line method:

_____

b. Double-declining-balance method:

First year: _____

Second year: _____

EXERCISE 10-14

a. Straight-line method:

First year: _____

Second year: _____

b. Double-declining-balance method:

First year: _____

Second year: _____

EXERCISE 10-15

a. _____

b. _____

c. _____

EXERCISE 10-16

a. and b.

JOURNAL

PAGE

	DATE		DESCRIPTION	POST. REF.	DEBIT	CREDIT	
1							1
2							2
3							3
4							4
5							5
6							6
7							7
8							8
9							9
10							10
11							11
12							12
13							13
14							14
15							15
16							16
17							17

EXERCISE 10-17

a.

b.(1) and (2)

JOURNAL   PAGE

	DATE	DESCRIPTION	POST. REF.	DEBIT	CREDIT	
1						1
2						2
3						3
4						4
5						5
6						6
7						7
8						8
9						9

EXERCISE 10-18

a. 2005: _____

  2006: _____

  2007: _____

b. _____

EXERCISE 10-18, Continued

c. and d.

JOURNAL PAGE

	DATE	DESCRIPTION	POST. REF.	DEBIT	CREDIT	
1						1
2						2
3						3
4						4
5						5
6						6
7						7
8						8
9						9
10						10
11						11
12						12
13						13
14						14
15						15
16						16
17						17

EXERCISE 10-19

a. _____

_____

b. _____

_____

EXERCISE 10-20

a. _____

_____

b. _____

_____

EXERCISE 10-21

a. and b.

JOURNAL   PAGE

	DATE	DESCRIPTION	POST. REF.	DEBIT	CREDIT	
1						1
2						2
3						3
4						4
5						5
6						6
7						7
8						8
9						9
10						10
11						11
12						12

EXERCISE 10-22

a. and b.

JOURNAL   PAGE

	DATE	DESCRIPTION	POST. REF.	DEBIT	CREDIT	
1						1
2						2
3						3
4						4
5						5
6						6
7						7
8						8
9						9
10						10
11						11
12						12

EXERCISE 10-23

a. _____

b. _____

EXERCISE 10-24

a. _____

_____

b.

JOURNAL   PAGE

	DATE		DESCRIPTION	POST. REF.	DEBIT	CREDIT	
1							1
2							2
3							3
4							4

EXERCISE 10-25

a. _____

_____

b.

JOURNAL   PAGE

	DATE		DESCRIPTION	POST. REF.	DEBIT	CREDIT	
1							1
2							2
3							3
4							4

EXERCISE 10-26

a.

	Current Year	Preceding Year

b.

EXERCISE 10-27

EXERCISE 10-28

a. and b.

EXERCISE 10-29

a.

Best Buy: _____

_____

Circuit City Stores, Inc: _____

_____

_____

_____

b.

_____

_____

_____

_____

_____

_____

_____

APPENDIX EXERCISE 10-30

First Year: _____

_____

Second Year.: _____

_____

APPENDIX EXERCISE 10-31

First year: _____

_____

Second year: _____

_____

APPENDIX EXERCISE 10-32

First year: _____

_____

Second year: _____

_____

_____

PROBLEM 10-1 ___

1. and 2.

Item	Land	Land Improvements	Building	Other Accounts
a.				
b.				
c.				
d.				
e.				
f.				
g.				
h.				
i.				
j.				
k.				
l.				
m.				
n.				
o.				
p.				
q.				
r.				
s.				
Total				

*Indicates receipt

3.

_____

_____

_____

This Page Not Used.

PROBLEM 10-2 ___

| | Depreciation Expense | | |
Year	a. Straight-Line Method	b. Units-of-Production Method	c. Double-declining-Balance Method
2006	_____	_____	_____
2007	_____	_____	_____
2008	_____	_____	_____
Total	_____	_____	_____

Calculations:

_____

_____

_____

_____

_____

_____

_____

_____

_____

_____

_____

_____

_____

_____

_____

_____

_____

_____

_____

_____

_____

_____

_____

This Page Not Used.

PROBLEM 10-3 ___

a.

STRAIGHT-LINE METHOD

Year	Calculations	Depreciation Expense
2006		
2007		
2008		
2009		

b.

UNITS-OF-PRODUCTION METHOD

Year	Calculations	Depreciation Expense
2006		
2007		
2008		
2009		

c.

DOUBLE-DECLINING-BALANCE METHOD

Year	Calculations	Depreciation Expense
2006		
2007		
2008		
2009		

This Page Not Used.

PROBLEM 10-4 ___

1. a.

STRAIGHT-LINE METHOD

Year	Depreciation Expense	Accumulated Depreciation, End of Year	Book Value, End of Year
1			
2			
3			
4			
5			

b.

DOUBLE-DECLINING-BALANCE METHOD

Year	Depreciation Expense	Accumulated Depreciation, End of Year	Book Value, End of Year
1			
2			
3			
4			
5			

2.

PROBLEM 10-4 ___, Concluded

3.

JOURNAL   PAGE

DATE	DESCRIPTION	POST. REF.	DEBIT	CREDIT
1				
2				
3				
4				
5				
6				
7				
8				
9				
10				
11				
12				
13				
14				

4.

JOURNAL   PAGE

DATE	DESCRIPTION	POST. REF.	DEBIT	CREDIT
1				
2				
3				
4				
5				
6				
7				
8				
9				
10				
11				
12				
13				
14				

PROBLEM 10-5 ___

JOURNAL

	DATE	DESCRIPTION	POST. REF.	DEBIT	CREDIT	
1						1
2						2
3						3
4						4
5						5
6						6
7						7
8						8
9						9
10						10
11						11
12						12
13						13
14						14
15						15
16						16
17						17
18						18
19						19
20						20
21						21
22						22
23						23
24						24
25						25
26						26
27						27
28						28
29						29
30						30
31						31
32						32
33						33
34						34
35						35
36						36

PROBLEM 10-5 ___ , Concluded

JOURNAL

	DATE	DESCRIPTION	POST. REF.	DEBIT	CREDIT	
1						1
2						2
3						3
4						4
5						5
6						6
7						7
8						8
9						9
10						10
11						11
12						12
13						13
14						14
15						15
16						16
17						17
18						18
19						19
20						20
21						21
22						22
23						23
24						24
25						25
26						26
27						27
28						28
29						29
30						30
31						31
32						32
33						33
34						34
35						35
36						36

PROBLEM 10-6 ___

1.

a. _____

_____

_____

b. _____

_____

_____

c. _____

_____

_____

2.

JOURNAL

PAGE

	DATE		DESCRIPTION	POST. REF.	DEBIT	CREDIT	
1							1
2							2
3							3
4							4
5							5
6							6
7							7
8							8
9							9
10							10
11							11
12							12

This Page Not Used.

EXERCISE 11-1

EXERCISE 11-2

a.(1) through b.(2)

JOURNAL   PAGE

	DATE		DESCRIPTION	POST. REF.	DEBIT	CREDIT	
1							1
2							2
3							3
4							4
5							5
6							6
7							7
8							8
9							9
10							10
11							11
12							12
13							13
14							14
15							15
16							16
17							17
18							18
19							19
20							20

EXERCISE 11-3

a. _____

_____

b. (1) _____

   (2) _____

c. _____

_____

_____

_____

_____

_____

_____

_____

_____

_____

_____

_____

_____

_____

EXERCISE 11-4

a. and b.

JOURNAL

PAGE

	DATE	DESCRIPTION	POST. REF.	DEBIT	CREDIT	
1						1
2						2
3						3
4						4
5						5
6						6
7						7
8						8
9						9
10						10
11						11
12						12
13						13
14						14

EXERCISE 11-5

a. and b.

JOURNAL   PAGE

	DATE		DESCRIPTION	POST. REF.	DEBIT	CREDIT	
1							1
2							2
3							3
4							4
5							5
6							6
7							7
8							8
9							9

EXERCISE 11-6

a.–c.

JOURNAL   PAGE

	DATE		DESCRIPTION	POST. REF.	DEBIT	CREDIT	
1							1
2							2
3							3
4							4
5							5
6							6
7							7
8							8
9							9
10							10
11							11
12							12

EXERCISE 11-7

a. _____

_____

b. _____

_____

c. _____

_____

EXERCISE 11-8

a.

b.

EXERCISE 11-9

	Consultant	Computer Programmer	Administrator
Regular earnings..	$	$	$
Overtime earnings..			
Gross pay..	$	$	$
Less: Social security tax	$	$	$
Medicare tax..			
Federal income tax withheld			
	$	$	$
Net pay..	$	$	$

EXERCISE 11-9, Concluded

Withholding Supporting Calculations

	Consultant	Computer Programmer	Administrator

EXERCISE 11-10

a.

EXERCISE 11-10

b. and c.

		JOURNAL			PAGE

	DATE	DESCRIPTION	POST. REF.	DEBIT	CREDIT
1					
2					
3					
4					
5					
6					
7					
8					
9					
10					
11					
12					

d. _____

_____

_____

_____

_____

_____

EXERCISE 11-11

a.

EXERCISE 11-11, Concluded

b.

JOURNAL   PAGE

	DATE	DESCRIPTION	POST. REF.	DEBIT	CREDIT	
1						1
2						2
3						3
4						4
5						5
6						6
7						7
8						8
9						9

EXERCISE 11-12

a.

JOURNAL   PAGE

	DATE	DESCRIPTION	POST. REF.	DEBIT	CREDIT	
1						1
2						2
3						3
4						4
5						5
6						6
7						7
8						8

b.

JOURNAL   PAGE

	DATE	DESCRIPTION	POST. REF.	DEBIT	CREDIT	
1						1
2						2
3						3
4						4
5						5
6						6
7						7
8						8

EXERCISE 11-13

a.

JOURNAL   PAGE

	DATE	DESCRIPTION	POST. REF.	DEBIT	CREDIT	
1						1
2						2
3						3
4						4
5						5
6						6
7						7
8						8
9						9

b.

JOURNAL   PAGE

	DATE	DESCRIPTION	POST. REF.	DEBIT	CREDIT	
1						1
2						2
3						3
4						4
5						5
6						6
7						7
8						8
9						9

EXERCISE 11-14

_____

_____

_____

_____

_____

_____

_____

_____

EXERCISE 11-15

a. _____

_____

_____

_____

_____

b. _____

_____

_____

_____

_____

c. _____

_____

_____

_____

_____

d. _____

_____

_____

_____

_____

e. _____

_____

_____

_____

EXERCISE 11-16

_____

_____

_____

_____

_____

_____

_____

_____

_____

_____

_____

_____

_____

EXERCISE 11-17

JOURNAL   PAGE

	DATE		DESCRIPTION	POST. REF.	DEBIT	CREDIT	
1							1
2							2
3							3

EXERCISE 11-18

a. and b.

JOURNAL   PAGE

	DATE		DESCRIPTION	POST. REF.	DEBIT	CREDIT	
1							1
2							2
3							3
4							4
5							5
6							6

EXERCISE 11-19

_____

_____

_____

_____

_____

_____

_____

_____

_____

_____

_____

_____

_____

_____

_____

_____

_____

EXERCISE 11-20

a. and b.

JOURNAL   PAGE

	DATE		DESCRIPTION	POST. REF.	DEBIT	CREDIT	
1							1
2							2
3							3
4							4
5							5
6							6

EXERCISE 11-21

a. _____

_____

_____

_____

_____

_____

_____

_____

b.

JOURNAL   PAGE

	DATE		DESCRIPTION	POST. REF.	DEBIT	CREDIT	
1							1
2							2
3							3
4							4

EXERCISE 11-22

a.

JOURNAL   *PAGE*

	DATE		DESCRIPTION	POST. REF.	DEBIT	CREDIT	
1							1
2							2
3							3
4							4

b. _____

_____

_____

_____

_____

_____

_____

_____

_____

EXERCISE 11-23

a. 2008: _____

_____

2007: _____

_____

b. _____

_____

_____

_____

_____

_____

_____

_____

_____

_____

_____

_____

_____

_____

_____

EXERCISE 11-24

a.

	Apple Computer Inc:	Dell Inc.:
Quick Ratio		

b. _____
_____
_____
_____
_____
_____
_____
_____
_____
_____
_____
_____
_____
_____
_____
_____

PROBLEM 11-1 ___

1.

JOURNAL   PAGE

	DATE		DESCRIPTION	POST. REF.	DEBIT	CREDIT	
1							1
2							2
3							3
4							4
5							5
6							6
7							7
8							8
9							9
10							10
11							11
12							12
13							13
14							14
15							15
16							16
17							17
18							18
19							19
20							20
21							21
22							22
23							23
24							24
25							25
26							26
27							27
28							28
29							29
30							30
31							31
32							32
33							33
34							34
35							35
36							36

PROBLEM 11-1 ___, Concluded

1. and 2.

JOURNAL

PAGE

	DATE		DESCRIPTION	POST. REF.	DEBIT	CREDIT	
1							1
2							2
3							3
4							4
5							5
6							6
7							7
8							8
9							9
10							10
11							11
12							12
13							13
14							14
15							15
16							16
17							17
18							18
19							19
20							20
21							21
22							22
23							23
24							24
25							25
26							26
27							27
28							28
29							29
30							30
31							31
32							32
33							33
34							34
35							35
36							36

PROBLEM 11-2 ___

1. and 2.

JOURNAL

PAGE

	DATE		DESCRIPTION	POST. REF.	DEBIT	CREDIT	
1							1
2							2
3							3
4							4
5							5
6							6
7							7
8							8
9							9
10							10
11							11
12							12
13							13
14							14
15							15
16							16
17							17
18							18
19							19
20							20
21							21
22							22
23							23
24							24
25							25
26							26
27							27
28							28
29							29
30							30
31							31
32							32
33							33
34							34
35							35
36							36

This Page Not Used.

PROBLEM 11-3 ___

1.

Employee	Gross Earnings	Federal Income Tax Withheld	Social Security Tax Withheld	Medicare Tax Withheld

_____

_____

_____

2. Payroll taxes incurred and paid by employer:

    a. Social security tax paid by employer............................ $ _____

    b. Medicare tax paid by employer .... _____

    c. State unemployment compensation tax........................ _____

    _____

    _____

    _____

    _____

    _____

    _____

    d. Federal unemployment compensation tax.................... _____

    e. Total payroll taxes expense .... $ _____

This Page Not Used.

463

PROBLEM 11-4 ___

PAYROLL FOR THE WEEK ENDED *December 12, 2008*

Name	Total Hours	EARNINGS			DEDUCTION					PAID		ACCOUNTS DEBITED		
		Regular	Over-time	Total	Social Security Tax	Medicare Tax	Federal Income Tax	Medical Insurance	Total	Net Amount	Ck. No.	Sales Salaries Expense	Office Salaries Expense	Delivery Salaries Expense
Alvarez, Julio	43.00	600.00	67.50	667.50	40.05	10.01	106.80	28.20	185.06	482.44	632	667.50		
Christy, T. Howard	45.00	480.00	90.00	570.00	34.20	8.55	85.50	46.70	174.95	395.05	633	570.00		
Davis, Lyn	40.00	720.00		720.00	43.20	10.80	104.40	26.30	184.70	535.30	634			720.00
Gunwald, Jenny		1,500.00		1,500.00	90.00	22.50	285.00	85.00	482.50	1,017.50	635		1,500.00	
Jenkins, Sara	46.00	840.00	189.00	1,029.00	61.74	15.44	180.08	75.00	332.26	696.74	636	1,029.00		
Ouchi, T.		1,400.00		1,400.00	84.00	21.00	252.00	95.00	452.00	948.00	637		1,400.00	
Peters, Ken	50.00	800.00	300.00	1,100.00	66.00	16.50	192.50	70.40	345.40	754.60	638		1,100.00	
Raines, Frank	47.00	720.00	189.00	909.00	54.54	13.64	154.53	24.50	247.21	661.79	639			909.00
Wilson, T. J.	38.00	330.00		330.00	19.80	4.95	41.25	18.10	84.10	245.90	640			330.00
		7,390.00	835.50	8,225.50	493.53	123.39	1,402.06	469.20	2,488.18	5,737.32		3,666.50	2,600.00	1,959.00

PROBLEM 11-4 ___, Continued

1.–4.

JOURNAL   PAGE

	DATE	DESCRIPTION	POST. REF.	DEBIT	CREDIT	
1						1
2						2
3						3
4						4
5						5
6						6
7						7
8						8
9						9
10						10
11						11
12						12
13						13
14						14
15						15
16						16
17						17
18						18
19						19
20						20
21						21
22						22
23						23
24						24
25						25
26						26
27						27
28						28
29						29
30						30
31						31
32						32
33						33
34						34
35						35
36						36

PROBLEM 11-5 ___

1. *The payroll register form is on pages 488.*

2.

JOURNAL   PAGE

	DATE		DESCRIPTION	POST. REF.	DEBIT	CREDIT	
1							1
2							2
3							3
4							4
5							5
6							6
7							7
8							8
9							9
10							10

PROBLEM 11-5 ___, Continued
1.

PAYROLL FOR WEEK ENDING

	NAME	TOTAL HOURS	EARNINGS			DEDUCTIONS		
			REGULAR	OVERTIME	TOTAL	SOCIAL SECURITY TAX	MEDICARE TAX	
1								1
2								2
3								3
4								4
5								5
6								6
7								7
8								8
9								9
10								10
11								11
12								12
13								13
14								14
15								15
16								16
17								17
18								18
19								19
20								20
21								21
22								22
23								23
24								24
25								25
26								26
27								27
28								28
29								29
30								30
31								31
32								32
33								33

PROBLEM 11-5 ____, Concluded

December 7, 2008

	FEDERAL INCOME TAX	U.S. SAVINGS BONDS	TOTAL	PAID NET AMOUNT	CK. NO.	ACCOUNTS DEBITED SALES SALARIES EXPENSE	OFFICE SALARIES EXPENSE	
1								1
2								2
3								3
4								4
5								5
6								6
7								7
8								8
9								9
10								10
11								11
12								12
13								13
14								14
15								15
16								16
17								17
18								18
19								19
20								20
21								21
22								22
23								23
24								24
25								25
26								26
27								27
28								28
29								29
30								30
31								31
32								32
33								33

This Page Not Used.

PROBLEM 11-6 ___

1.

JOURNAL   PAGE

	DATE		DESCRIPTION	POST. REF.	DEBIT	CREDIT	
1							1
2							2
3							3
4							4
5							5
6							6
7							7
8							8
9							9
10							10
11							11
12							12
13							13
14							14
15							15
16							16
17							17
18							18
19							19
20							20
21							21
22							22
23							23
24							24
25							25
26							26
27							27
28							28
29							29
30							30
31							31
32							32
33							33
34							34
35							35
36							36

PROBLEM 11-6 ___, Continued

JOURNAL   PAGE _____

	DATE		DESCRIPTION	POST. REF.	DEBIT	CREDIT	
1							1
2							2
3							3
4							4
5							5
6							6
7							7
8							8
9							9
10							10
11							11
12							12
13							13
14							14
15							15
16							16
17							17
18							18
19							19
20							20
21							21
22							22
23							23
24							24
25							25
26							26
27							27
28							28
29							29
30							30
31							31
32							32
33							33
34							34
35							35
36							36

PROBLEM 11-6 ___, Concluded

2.

JOURNAL

PAGE

	DATE		DESCRIPTION	POST. REF.	DEBIT	CREDIT	
1							1
2							2
3							3
4							4
5							5
6							6
7							7
8							8
9							9
10							10
11							11
12							12
13							13
14							14
15							15
16							16
17							17
18							18
19							19
20							20
21							21
22							22
23							23
24							24
25							25
26							26
27							27
28							28
29							29
30							30
31							31
32							32
33							33
34							34
35							35
36							36

This Page Not Used.

COMPREHENSIVE PROBLEM 3

1.

JOURNAL   PAGE

	DATE		DESCRIPTION	POST. REF.	DEBIT	CREDIT	
1							1
2							2
3							3
4							4
5							5
6							6
7							7
8							8
9							9
10							10
11							11
12							12
13							13
14							14
15							15
16							16
17							17
18							18
19							19
20							20
21							21
22							22
23							23
24							24
25							25
26							26
27							27
28							28
29							29
30							30
31							31
32							32
33							33
34							34
35							35
36							36

COMPREHENSIVE PROBLEM 3, Continued

JOURNAL　　　　　　　　　　　　　　PAGE _____

	DATE		DESCRIPTION	POST. REF.	DEBIT	CREDIT	
1							1
2							2
3							3
4							4
5							5
6							6
7							7
8							8
9							9
10							10
11							11
12							12
13							13
14							14
15							15
16							16
17							17
18							18
19							19
20							20
21							21
22							22
23							23
24							24
25							25
26							26
27							27
28							28
29							29
30							30
31							31
32							32
33							33
34							34
35							35
36							36

COMPREHENSIVE PROBLEM 3, Continued

2.

COMPREHENSIVE PROBLEM 3, Continued

3. and 4.

JOURNAL   PAGE

	DATE		DESCRIPTION	POST. REF.	DEBIT	CREDIT	
1							1
2							2
3							3
4							4
5							5
6							6
7							7
8							8
9							9
10							10
11							11
12							12
13							13
14							14
15							15
16							16
17							17
18							18
19							19
20							20
21							21
22							22
23							23
24							24
25							25
26							26
27							27
28							28
29							29
30							30
31							31
32							32
33							33
34							34
35							35
36							36

COMPREHENSIVE PROBLEM 3, Continued

JOURNAL

	DATE		DESCRIPTION	POST. REF.	DEBIT	CREDIT	
1							1
2							2
3							3
4							4
5							5
6							6
7							7
8							8
9							9
10							10
11							11
12							12
13							13
14							14
15							15
16							16
17							17
18							18
19							19
20							20
21							21
22							22
23							23
24							24
25							25
26							26
27							27
28							28
29							29
30							30
31							31
32							32
33							33
34							34
35							35
36							36

Name _____

COMPREHENSIVE PROBLEM 3, Continued

5. *Omit "00" in the cents columns.*

COMPREHENSIVE PROBLEM 3, Concluded

6.

EXERCISE 12-1

JOURNAL

PAGE

	DATE		DESCRIPTION	POST. REF.	DEBIT	CREDIT	
1							1
2							2
3							3
4							4
5							5
6							6

EXERCISE 12-2

JOURNAL

PAGE

	DATE		DESCRIPTION	POST. REF.	DEBIT	CREDIT	
1							1
2							2
3							3
4							4
5							5
6							6
7							7
8							8
9							9

EXERCISE 12-3

	Haley	Manos
a.	_____	_____
b.	_____	_____
c.	_____	_____
d.	_____	_____
e.	_____	_____

Details

	Haley	Manos	Total
a.			
b.			
c.			
d.			
e.			

EXERCISE 12-4

	Haley	Manos
a.	_____	_____
b.	_____	_____
c.	_____	_____
d.	_____	_____
e.	_____	_____

Details

	Haley	Manos	Total
a.			
b.			
c.			
d.			
e.			

EXERCISE   12-5

	Curt Kelly	Greg Kaufman	Total

EXERCISE 12-6

_____

_____

_____

_____

_____

_____

_____

_____

_____

_____

_____

_____

EXERCISE 12-7

	Gardner	Ross	Total
a.			

EXERCISE 12-7 Concluded

b. (1) and (2)

JOURNAL

	DATE	DESCRIPTION	POST. REF.	DEBIT	CREDIT	
1						1
2						2
3						3
4						4
5						5
6						6
7						7
8						8
9						9
10						10
11						11

EXERCISE 12-8

a.

	KXT Radio Partners	Rachel Sizemore	Daily Sun Newspaper LLC	Total

EXERCISE 12-8 Concluded

b.

JOURNAL

	DATE	DESCRIPTION	POST. REF.	DEBIT	CREDIT	
1						1
2						2
3						3
4						4
5						5
6						6
7						7
8						8
9						9
10						10
11						11
12						12

c. *Omit "00" in the cents columns.*

Statement of Members' Equity

	KXT Radio Partners	Rachel Sizemore	Daily Sun Newspaper, LLC	Total

EXERCISE 12-9

a. – c.

JOURNAL PAGE

	DATE		DESCRIPTION	POST. REF.	DEBIT	CREDIT	
1							1
2							2
3							3
4							4
5							5
6							6
7							7
8							8
9							9
10							10
11							11
12							12

EXERCISE 12-10

a. and b.

JOURNAL PAGE

	DATE		DESCRIPTION	POST. REF.	DEBIT	CREDIT	
1							1
2							2
3							3

_____

_____

_____

EXERCISE 12-11

a. _____

b. _____

c. _____

_____

_____

EXERCISE 12-12

a. (1) and (2)

JOURNAL   PAGE

	DATE		DESCRIPTION	POST. REF.	DEBIT	CREDIT	
1							1
2							2
3							3
4							4
5							5
6							6
7							7
8							8

b. _____

_____

_____

_____

_____

EXERCISE 12-13

a.

JOURNAL   PAGE

	DATE		DESCRIPTION	POST. REF.	DEBIT	CREDIT	
1							1
2							2
3							3
4							4
5							5
6							6
7							7
8							8

b. _____

_____

_____

_____

_____

EXERCISE 12-14

a. and b. (1) and (2)

JOURNAL   PAGE

	DATE	DESCRIPTION	POST. REF.	DEBIT	CREDIT	
1						1
2						2
3						3
4						4
5						5
6						6
7						7
8						8
9						9
10						10
11						11
12						12
13						13

Supporting calculations for the bonus:

EXERCISE 12-14, Continued

JOURNAL   PAGE _____

	DATE	DESCRIPTION	POST. REF.	DEBIT	CREDIT	
1						1
2						2
3						3
4						4

Supporting calculations for the bonus:

EXERCISE 12-15

JOURNAL   PAGE

	DATE	DESCRIPTION	POST. REF.	DEBIT	CREDIT	
1						1
2						2
3						3
4						4
5						5
6						6
7						7
8						8

Supporting Calculations for the bonus:

JOURNAL   PAGE

	DATE	DESCRIPTION	POST. REF.	DEBIT	CREDIT	
1						1
2						2
3						3
4						4

Supporting calculations for the bonus:

EXERCISE 12-16

Omit "00" in the cents columns.

Statement of Partnership Equity

	Jan Strous, Capital	Lisa Lankford, Capital	Sara Rogers, Capital	Total Partnership Capital

<u>Calculations</u>
Admission of Sarah Rogers:

_____

_____

_____

_____

_____

_____

_____

Net income distribution:

_____

_____

_____

_____

_____

_____

_____

Withdrawals:

_____

_____

_____

_____

_____

EXERCISE 12-17

a. and b.

JOURNAL   PAGE _____

	DATE		DESCRIPTION	POST. REF.	DEBIT	CREDIT	
1							1
2							2
3							3
4							4
5							5
6							6
7							7
8							8
9							9
10							10
11							11
12							12

EXERCISE 12-18

a. – e.

EXERCISE 12-18, Concluded

EXERCISE 12-19

a.

b. and c.

		Pitt		Leon	

EXERCISE 12-20

	Boling	Bishop

EXERCISE 12-21

a. _____

b. _____

c.

JOURNAL   PAGE

	DATE	DESCRIPTION	POST. REF.	DEBIT	CREDIT	
1						1
2						2
3						3

Supporting calculations:

		Mawby	White	Shelby	
1					1
2					2
3					3
4					4

EXERCISE 12-22

a.

	Seth	Kerr	Driver	Total	
1					1
2					2
3					3
4					4
5					5
6					6
7					7

b.

	Seth	Kerr	Driver	Total	
1					1
2					2
3					3
4					4
5					5
6					6
7					7
8					8
9					9

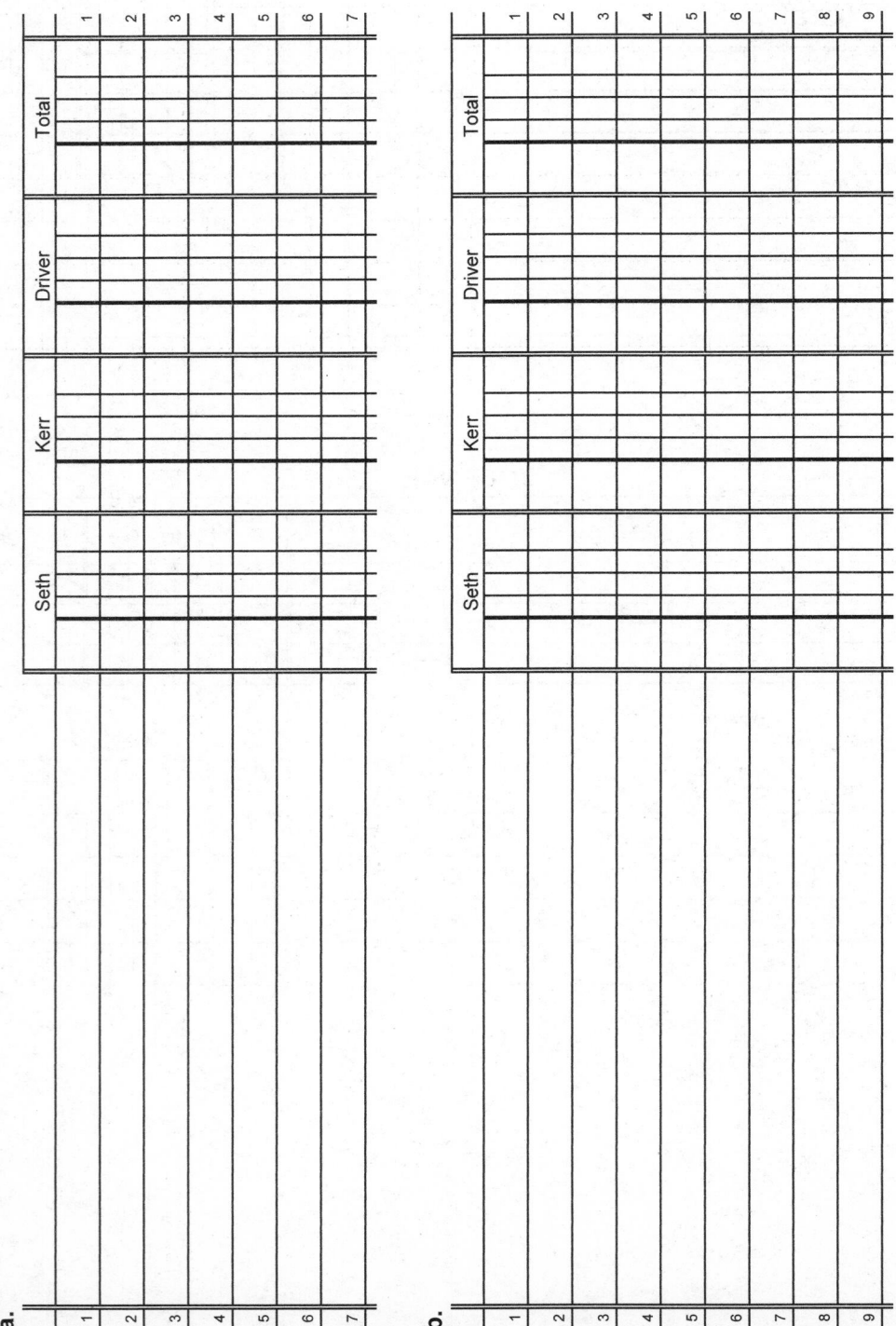

EXERCISE 12-23

	Heinz	Dicer	Ho	
1				1
2				2
3				3
4				4
5				5
6				6
7				7
8				8
9				9
10				10
11				11
12				12
13				13
14				14

Chapter 12

EXERCISE 12-24

Omit "00" in the cents columns.

Dills, Gordon, and Chavez

Statement of Partnership Liquidation

For the Period Ending July 1–29, 20--

	CASH	NONCASH ASSETS	LIABILITIES	CAPITAL		
				DILLS	GORDON	CHAVEZ

EXERCISE   12-25

a. *Omit "00" in the cents columns.*

City Signs, LLC

Statement of LLC Liquidation

For the Period March 1–31, 2008

	CASH	NONCASH ASSETS	LIABILITIES +	MEMBER EQUITY		
				GILLEY	HUGHES	MOUSSA

EXERCISE 12-25, Concluded

b.

	DATE	DESCRIPTION	POST. REF.	DEBIT	CREDIT

JOURNAL   PAGE

	DATE	DESCRIPTION	POST. REF.	DEBIT	CREDIT	
1						1
2						2
3						3
4						4
5						5
6						6
7						7
8						8
9						9
10						10
11						11
12						12

EXERCISE 12-26

a.

JOURNAL PAGE

	DATE		DESCRIPTION	POST. REF.	DEBIT	CREDIT	
1							1
2							2
3							3
4							4
5							5
6							6
7							7
8							8
9							9
10							10
11							11
12							12

b. *Omit "00" in cents columns.*

Statement of Partnership Equity

	Dal Polivka	Amanda Pratt	Total

EXERCISE 12-27

a.

b.

EXERCISE 12-28

a.

b.

504

This Page Not Used.

PROBLEM 12-1___

1.

	DATE		DESCRIPTION	POST. REF.	DEBIT	CREDIT	
1							1
2							2
3							3
4							4
5							5
6							6
7							7
8							8
9							9
10							10
11							11

JOURNAL   PAGE

2.

Balance Sheet

PROBLEM 12-1___, Concluded

3.

1.

| | JOURNAL | | | PAGE |

	DATE	DESCRIPTION	POST. REF.	DEBIT	CREDIT	
1						1
2						2
3						3
4						4
5						5
6						6
7						7
8						8
9						9
10						10
11						11
12						12
13						13
14						14
15						15
16						16
17						17
18						18

Supporting calculations:

PROBLEM 12-2___

	(1) Net Income of		(2) Net Income of	
Plan				
a.				
b.				
c.				
d.				
e.				
f.				

Supporting calculations:

This Page Not Used.

PROBLEM 12-3

Omit "00" in the cents columns.

1.

Income Statement

Division of Net Income

PROBLEM 12-3___, Continued

Omit "00" in cents columns.

2. _____

Statement of Partners' Equity

PROBLEM 12-3___, Concluded

3. _____

_____

Balance Sheet

512

This Page Not Used.

PROBLEM 12-4 ___

1. and 2.   **JOURNAL**   PAGE

	DATE		DESCRIPTION	POST. REF.	DEBIT	CREDIT	
1							1
2							2
3							3
4							4
5							5
6							6
7							7
8							8
9							9
10							10
11							11
12							12
13							13
14							14
15							15
16							16
17							17
18							18
19							19
20							20
21							21
22							22
23							23
24							24
25							25
26							26
27							27
28							28
29							29
30							30
31							31
32							32
33							33
34							34
35							35
36							36
37							37

PROBLEM 12-4___, Concluded

3. *Omit "00" in the cents columns.*

Balance Sheet

PROBLEM 12-5 _____

1. Omit "00" in the cents columns.

Statement of Partnership Liquidation

	CASH	NONCASH ASSETS	LIABILITIES +	CAPITAL

PROBLEM 12-5___, Concluded

2.

PROBLEM 12-6

1. Omit "00" in the cents columns.

Statement of Partnership Liquidation

	CASH	NONCASH ASSETS	LIABILITIES	CAPITAL

PROBLEM 12-6____, Concluded

2. Omit "00" in the cents columns.

Statement of Partnership Liquidation

CASH	NONCASH ASSETS	LIABILITIES	CAPITAL	

EXERCISE 13-1

Description	1st Year	2nd Year	3rd Year	4th Year
Total Dividend Declared				
Preferred Dividend				
Preferred Shares Outstanding				
Preferred Dividend per Share				
Dividend for Common Shares				
Common Shares Outstanding				
Common Dividend per Share				

EXERCISE 13-2

Description	1st Year	2nd Year	3rd Year	4th Year
Total Dividend Declared				
Preferred Dividend				
Preferred Shares Outstanding				
Preferred Dividend per Share				
Dividend for Common Shares				
Common Shares Outstanding				
Common Dividend per Share				

EXERCISE 13-3

a.

JOURNAL   PAGE

	DATE	DESCRIPTION	POST. REF.	DEBIT	CREDIT	
1						1
2						2
3						3
4						4
5						5
6						6
7						7
8						8
9						9
10						10
11						11

b. _____

EXERCISE 13-4

a.

JOURNAL PAGE _____

	DATE	DESCRIPTION	POST. REF.	DEBIT	CREDIT	
1						1
2						2
3						3
4						4
5						5
6						6
7						7
8						8
9						9
10						10
11						11
12						12
13						13
14						14
15						15
16						16
17						17
18						18

b. _____

EXERCISE 13-5

JOURNAL PAGE _____

	DATE	DESCRIPTION	POST. REF.	DEBIT	CREDIT	
1						1
2						2
3						3
4						4
5						5
6						6
7						7
8						8
9						9
10						10

EXERCISE 13-6

a.–c.

JOURNAL
PAGE

	DATE		DESCRIPTION	POST. REF.	DEBIT	CREDIT	
1							1
2							2
3							3
4							4
5							5
6							6
7							7
8							8
9							9
10							10
11							11
12							12
13							13
14							14
15							15
16							16
17							17
18							18

EXERCISE 13-7

JOURNAL
PAGE

	DATE		DESCRIPTION	POST. REF.	DEBIT	CREDIT	
1							1
2							2
3							3
4							4
5							5
6							6
7							7
8							8
9							9
10							10
11							11
12							12

EXERCISE 13-8

JOURNAL   PAGE

	DATE	DESCRIPTION	POST. REF.	DEBIT	CREDIT	
1						1
2						2
3						3
4						4
5						5
6						6
7						7
8						8
9						9
10						10
11						11
12						12
13						13
14						14
15						15
16						16
17						17
18						18

EXERCISE 13-9

JOURNAL   PAGE

	DATE	DESCRIPTION	POST. REF.	DEBIT	CREDIT	
1						1
2						2
3						3
4						4
5						5
6						6
7						7
8						8
9						9

EXERCISE 13-10

a. (1) and (2)

JOURNAL   PAGE _____

	DATE		DESCRIPTION	POST. REF.	DEBIT	CREDIT	
1							1
2							2
3							3
4							4
5							5
6							6
7							7
8							8
9							9

b. (1) Total paid-in capital: _____

   (2) Total retained earnings: _____

   (3) Total stockholders' equity: _____

c. (1) Total paid-in capital: _____

   (2) Total retained earnings: _____

   (3) Total stockholders' equity: _____

EXERCISE 13-11

a.

JOURNAL   PAGE _____

	DATE		DESCRIPTION	POST. REF.	DEBIT	CREDIT	
1							1
2							2
3							3
4							4
5							5
6							6
7							7
8							8
9							9
10							10
11							11
12							12
13							13

EXERCISE 13-11, Concluded

b. _____

c. _____

_____

_____

_____

_____

_____

_____

EXERCISE 13-12

a.

JOURNAL   PAGE

	DATE	DESCRIPTION	POST. REF.	DEBIT	CREDIT	
1						1
2						2
3						3
4						4
5						5
6						6
7						7
8						8
9						9
10						10
11						11
12						12
13						13
14						14
15						15

b. _____

c. _____

d. _____

_____

_____

_____

_____

_____

EXERCISE 13-13

a.

JOURNAL PAGE

	DATE		DESCRIPTION	POST. REF.	DEBIT	CREDIT	
1							1
2							2
3							3
4							4
5							5
6							6
7							7
8							8
9							9
10							10
11							11
12							12
13							13
14							14
15							15
16							16
17							17
18							18
19							19

b. _____

c. _____

d. _____

_____

_____

_____

_____

_____

_____

_____

_____

EXERCISE 13-14

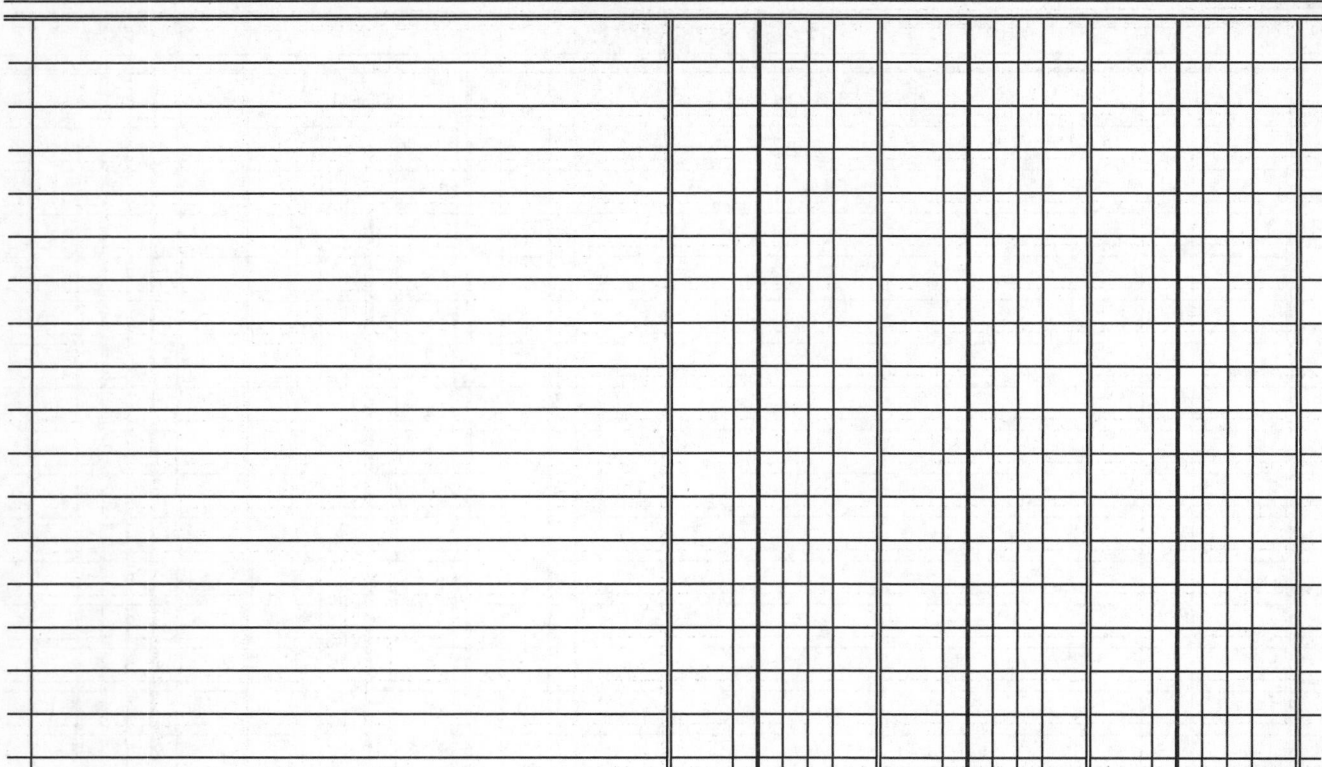

EXERCISE 13-15

EXERCISE 13-16

EXERCISE 13-17

EXERCISE 13-18

EXERCISE 13-20

a. _____

b. _____

EXERCISE 13-21

	Assets	Liabilities	Stockholders' Equity
(1) Declaring a cash dividend	_____	_____	_____
(2) Paying the cash dividend declared in (1)	_____	_____	_____
(3) Authorizing and issuing stock certificates in a stock split...	_____	_____	_____
(4) Declaring a stock dividend	_____	_____	_____
(5) Issuing stock certificates for the stock dividend declared in (4)......................................	_____	_____	_____

EXERCISE 13-22

JOURNAL   PAGE

	DATE		DESCRIPTION	POST. REF.	DEBIT	CREDIT	
1							1
2							2
3							3
4							4
5							5
6							6
7							7
8							8
9							9
10							10
11							11
12							12
13							13
14							14
15							15
16							16
17							17
18							18
19							19
20							20
21							21
22							22
23							23
24							24
25							25

EXERCISE 13-23

EXERCISE 13-24

a. _____

b. _____

EXERCISE 13-25

PROBLEM 13-1 ___

1.

Year	Total Dividends	Preferred Dividends		Common Dividends	
		Total	Per Share	Total	Per Share
2003					
2004					
2005					
2006					
2007					
2008					

2.

_____

_____

3.

_____

_____

_____

This Page Not Used.

PROBLEM 13-2 ___

JOURNAL

PAGE ___

	DATE		DESCRIPTION	POST. REF.	DEBIT	CREDIT	
1							1
2							2
3							3
4							4
5							5
6							6
7							7
8							8
9							9
10							10
11							11
12							12
13							13
14							14
15							15
16							16
17							17
18							18
19							19
20							20
21							21
22							22
23							23
24							24
25							25
26							26
27							27
28							28
29							29
30							30
31							31
32							32
33							33
34							34
35							35
36							36

This Page Not Used.

PROBLEM 13-3 ___

a.–g.

JOURNAL

	DATE		DESCRIPTION	POST. REF.	DEBIT	CREDIT	
1							1
2							2
3							3
4							4
5							5
6							6
7							7
8							8
9							9
10							10
11							11
12							12
13							13
14							14
15							15
16							16
17							17
18							18
19							19
20							20
21							21
22							22
23							23
24							24
25							25
26							26
27							27
28							28
29							29
30							30
31							31
32							32
33							33
34							34
35							35
36							36

538

This Page Not Used.

PROBLEM 13-4 ___

1. and 2.

Common Stock

Paid-In Capital in Excess of Stated Value

Retained Earnings

Treasury Stock

Paid-In Capital from Sale of Treasury Stock

PROBLEM 13-4 ___, Continued

Stock Dividends Distributable

Stock Dividends

Cash Dividends

PROBLEM 13-4 ___, Continued

2.

JOURNAL

PAGE

	DATE		DESCRIPTION	POST. REF.	DEBIT	CREDIT	
1							1
2							2
3							3
4							4
5							5
6							6
7							7
8							8
9							9
10							10
11							11
12							12
13							13
14							14
15							15
16							16
17							17
18							18
19							19
20							20
21							21
22							22
23							23
24							24
25							25
26							26
27							27
28							28
29							29
30							30
31							31
32							32
33							33
34							34
35							35
36							36

PROBLEM 13-4 ___, Concluded

3.

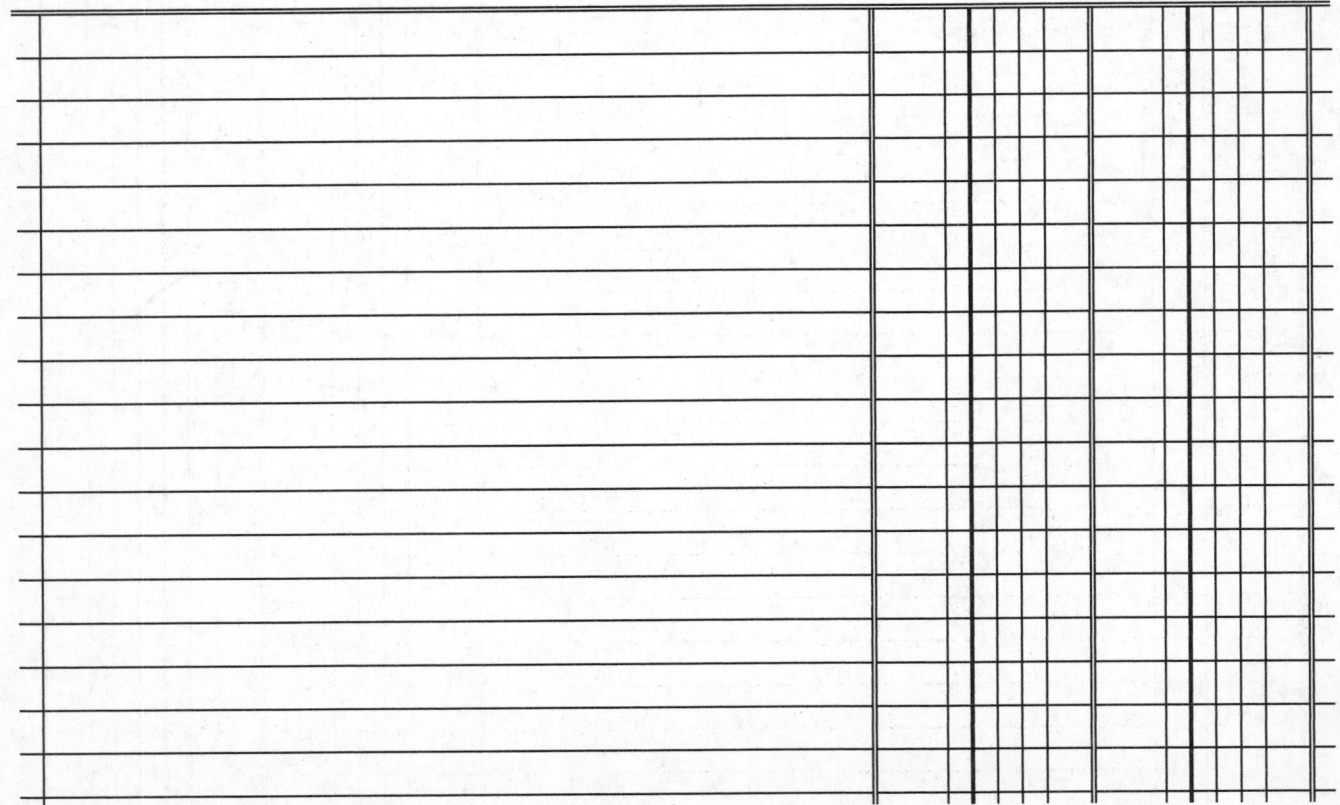

4.

PROBLEM 13-5 ___

JOURNAL

	DATE		DESCRIPTION	POST. REF.	DEBIT	CREDIT	
1							1
2							2
3							3
4							4
5							5
6							6
7							7
8							8
9							9
10							10
11							11
12							12
13							13
14							14
15							15
16							16
17							17
18							18
19							19
20							20
21							21
22							22
23							23
24							24
25							25
26							26
27							27
28							28
29							29
30							30
31							31
32							32
33							33
34							34
35							35
36							36

PROBLEM 13-5 ___, Concluded

JOURNAL

	DATE	DESCRIPTION	POST. REF.	DEBIT	CREDIT	
1						1
2						2
3						3
4						4
5						5
6						6
7						7
8						8
9						9
10						10
11						11
12						12
13						13
14						14
15						15
16						16
17						17
18						18
19						19
20						20
21						21
22						22
23						23
24						24
25						25
26						26
27						27
28						28
29						29
30						30
31						31
32						32
33						33
34						34
35						35
36						36

EXERCISE 14-1

JOURNAL

PAGE

	DATE		DESCRIPTION	POST. REF.	DEBIT	CREDIT	
1							1
2							2
3							3
4							4
5							5
6							6
7							7
8							8
9							9
10							10
11							11
12							12
13							13
14							14
15							15
16							16
17							17
18							18

EXERCISE 14-2

JOURNAL

PAGE

	DATE		DESCRIPTION	POST. REF.	DEBIT	CREDIT	
1							1
2							2
3							3
4							4
5							5
6							6
7							7
8							8
9							9
10							10
11							11
12							12
13							13
14							14
15							15

EXERCISE 14-3

JOURNAL

PAGE

	DATE		DESCRIPTION	POST. REF.	DEBIT	CREDIT	
1							1
2							2
3							3
4							4
5							5
6							6
7							7
8							8
9							9
10							10
11							11
12							12
13							13
14							14
15							15

EXERCISE 14-4

a.

_____
_____
_____
_____
_____
_____
_____
_____
_____
_____
_____
_____

b.

JOURNAL   PAGE

	DATE		DESCRIPTION	POST. REF.	DEBIT	CREDIT	
1							1
2							2
3							3
4							4
5							5

c.

_____
_____

EXERCISE 14-5

a.

JOURNAL   PAGE

	DATE		DESCRIPTION	POST. REF.	DEBIT	CREDIT	
1							1
2							2
3							3
4							4
5							5
6							6

b.

_____

_____

_____

_____

_____

_____

_____

_____

EXERCISE 14-6

a.

JOURNAL					PAGE

	DATE	DESCRIPTION	POST. REF.	DEBIT	CREDIT	
1						1
2						2
3						3
4						4
5						5
6						6
7						7
8						8

b.

JOURNAL					PAGE

	DATE	DESCRIPTION	POST. REF.	DEBIT	CREDIT	
1						1
2						2
3						3
4						4
5						5
6						6
7						7
8						8

c. Balance sheet disclosure:

EXERCISE 14-6, Concluded

Note disclosure:

_____

_____

_____

_____

_____

_____

_____

_____

_____

_____

EXERCISE 14-7

a.

EXERCISE 14-7, Concluded

b.

JOURNAL   PAGE

	DATE		DESCRIPTION	POST. REF.	DEBIT	CREDIT	
1							1
2							2
3							3

c.

JOURNAL   PAGE

	DATE		DESCRIPTION	POST. REF.	DEBIT	CREDIT	
1							1
2							2
3							3

d. Balance Sheet disclosure:

_____

_____

_____

_____

_____

e. Note disclosure:

_____

_____

_____

_____

_____

_____

EXERCISE 14-8

a. and c.

JOURNAL

PAGE

	DATE		DESCRIPTION	POST. REF.	DEBIT	CREDIT	
1							1
2							2
3							3
4							4
5							5
6							6
7							7
8							8
9							9

b. Balance sheet disclosure:

Note disclosure:

_____

_____

_____

_____

_____

_____

_____

_____

_____

_____

_____

EXERCISE 14-9

EXERCISE 14-10

EXERCISE 14-11

a.-c.

EXERCISE 14-12

a. _____   e. _____

b. _____   f. _____

c. _____   g. _____

d. _____   h. _____

EXERCISE 14-13

EXERCISE 14-14

EXERCISE 14-15

EXERCISE 14-16

a. – b.

EXERCISE 14-17

a. _____   e. _____

b. _____   f. _____

c. _____   g. _____

d. _____   h. _____

EXERCISE 14-18

a. _____

b. _____

EXERCISE 14-19

a.

b.

c.

EXERCISE 14-20

a. and b.

JOURNAL   PAGE

	DATE		DESCRIPTION	POST. REF.	DEBIT	CREDIT	
1							1
2							2
3							3
4							4
5							5
6							6
7							7
8							8

EXERCISE 14-21

a.

EXERCISE 14-21, Concluded

b.

EXERCISE 14-22

a.–c.

JOURNAL PAGE

	DATE	DESCRIPTION	POST. REF.	DEBIT	CREDIT	
1						1
2						2
3						3
4						4
5						5
6						6
7						7
8						8
9						9
10						10
11						11
12						12
13						13

EXERCISE 14-23

a. and b.

	JOURNAL				PAGE
DATE	DESCRIPTION	POST. REF.	DEBIT	CREDIT	
1					1
2					2
3					3
4					4
5					5
6					6
7					7

EXERCISE 14-24

EXERCISE 14-25

Earnings per Share:

_____

_____

_____

_____

_____

_____

_____

_____

Price-Earnings Ratio:

_____

_____

_____

_____

_____

_____

_____

_____

_____

_____

EXERCISE 14-26

a.

_____

Price-earnings ratio, 2005:

_____

_____

_____

Price-earnings ratio, 2004

_____

_____

Price-earnings ratio, 2003:

_____

EXERCISE 14-26, Concluded

b.

_____

_____

_____

_____

_____

_____

_____

_____

_____

_____

_____

_____

_____

_____

PROBLEM 14-1 ___

1. and 2.

Year	Income Tax Deducted on Income Statement	Income Tax Payments for the Year	Deferred Income Tax Payable	
			Year's Addition (Deduction)	Year-End Balance
First				
Second				
Third				
Fourth				
Total				

566

This Page Not Used.

PROBLEM 14-2 ___

Omit "00" in the cents columns.

PROBLEM 14-2 ___ , Concluded

PROBLEM 14-3 ___

1.

PROBLEM 14-3 ___ , Continued

2.

PROBLEM 14-3 ___, Continued

3.

PROBLEM 14-3 ___, Concluded

PROBLEM 14-4 ___

JOURNAL

PAGE

	DATE		DESCRIPTION	POST. REF.	DEBIT	CREDIT	
1							1
2							2
3							3
4							4
5							5
6							6
7							7
8							8
9							9
10							10
11							11
12							12
13							13
14							14
15							15
16							16
17							17
18							18
19							19
20							20
21							21
22							22
23							23
24							24
25							25
26							26
27							27
28							28
29							29
30							30
31							31
32							32
33							33
34							34
35							35
36							36

This Page Not Used.

EXERCISE 15-1

	(a)	(b)	(c)
Earnings before bond interest and income tax			
Bond interest			
Balance			
Income tax			
Net income			
Dividends on preferred stock			
Earnings available for common stock			
Earnings per share on common stock			

EXERCISE 15-2

_____
_____
_____
_____
_____
_____
_____
_____
_____
_____

EXERCISE 15-3

_____
_____
_____
_____
_____
_____
_____
_____

EXERCISE 15-4

a. _____

_____

_____

_____

_____

b. _____

EXERCISE 15-5

a. _____

_____

_____

_____

_____

_____

b. _____

EXERCISE 15-6

_____

_____

EXERCISE 15-7

_____

_____

_____

_____

_____

_____

_____

_____

_____

EXERCISE 15-8

EXERCISE 15-9

EXERCISE 15-10

EXERCISE 15-11

JOURNAL   PAGE

	DATE		DESCRIPTION	POST. REF.	DEBIT	CREDIT	
1							1
2							2
3							3
4							4
5							5
6							6
7							7
8							8
9							9
10							10

EXERCISE 15-12

a. 1.–4.

JOURNAL   PAGE

	DATE		DESCRIPTION	POST. REF.	DEBIT	CREDIT	
1							1
2							2
3							3
4							4
5							5
6							6
7							7
8							8
9							9
10							10
11							11
12							12
13							13
14							14
15							15

EXERCISE 15-12, Concluded

b.

EXERCISE 15-13

a. and b.

JOURNAL   PAGE

	DATE	DESCRIPTION	POST. REF.	DEBIT	CREDIT	
1						1
2						2
3						3
4						4
5						5
6						6
7						7

Supporting calculations

EXERCISE 15-14

JOURNAL   PAGE

	DATE		DESCRIPTION	POST. REF.	DEBIT	CREDIT	
1							1
2							2
3							3
4							4
5							5
6							6
7							7
8							8
9							9
10							10
11							11
12							12
13							13
14							14
15							15
16							16

EXERCISE 15-15

JOURNAL   PAGE

	DATE		DESCRIPTION	POST. REF.	DEBIT	CREDIT	
1							1
2							2
3							3
4							4
5							5
6							6
7							7
8							8
9							9
10							10
11							11
12							12
13							12
14							14
15							15
16							16

EXERCISE 15-16

_____
_____
_____
_____
_____
_____
_____
_____

EXERCISE 15-17

_____
_____
_____
_____
_____

EXERCISE 15-18

a.–d.

JOURNAL   PAGE

	DATE	DESCRIPTION	POST. REF.	DEBIT	CREDIT	
1						1
2						2
3						3
4						4
5						5
6						6
7						7
8						8
9						9
10						10
11						11
12						12
13						13
14						14
15						15

EXERCISE 15-19

a.–d.

JOURNAL   PAGE

	DATE	DESCRIPTION	POST. REF.	DEBIT	CREDIT	
1						1
2						2
3						3
4						4
5						5
6						6
7						7
8						8
9						9
10						10
11						11
12						12
13						13
14						14
15						15
16						16
17						17

EXERCISE 15-20

a. Current year: _____

_____

_____

Preceding year: _____

_____

_____

b. _____

_____

_____

_____

_____

_____

_____

_____

APPENDIX EXERCISE 15-21

a. 1.–4.

JOURNAL   PAGE

	DATE		DESCRIPTION	POST. REF.	DEBIT	CREDIT	
1							1
2							2
3							3
4							4
5							5
6							6
7							7
8							8
9							9
10							10
11							11
12							12
13							13

Supporting calculations:

b.

APPENDIX EXERCISE 15-22

a. 1.–4.

JOURNAL   PAGE

	DATE	DESCRIPTION	POST. REF.	DEBIT	CREDIT	
1						1
2						2
3						3
4						4
5						5
6						6
7						7
8						8
9						9
10						10
11						11
12						12
13						13
14						14
15						15

Supporting calculations:

b.

APPENDIX EXERCISE 15-23

a.–d.

APPENDIX EXERCISE 15-24

a.–d.

PROBLEM 15-1 ___

1.

	Plan 1	Plan 2	Plan 3
Earnings before interest and income tax			
Deduct interest on bonds			
Income before income tax			
Deduct income tax			
Net income			
Dividends on preferred stock			
Available for dividends on common stock			
Shares of common stock outstanding			
Earnings per share on common stock			

2.

	Plan 1	Plan 2	Plan 3
Earnings before interest and income tax			
Deduct interest on bonds			
Income before income tax			
Deduct income tax			
Net income			
Dividends on preferred stock			
Available for dividends on common stock			
Shares of common stock outstanding			
Earnings per share on common stock			

PROBLEM 15-1 ___, Concluded

3.

PROBLEM 15-2 ___

1. and 2.

JOURNAL   PAGE

	DATE		DESCRIPTION	POST. REF.	DEBIT	CREDIT	
1							1
2							2
3							3
4							4
5							5
6							6
7							7
8							8
9							9
10							10
11							11
12							12
13							13
14							14
15							15
16							16
17							17
18							18
19							19
20							20
21							21
22							22
23							23
24							24
25							25

3.

_____

_____

_____

4.

_____

_____

_____

_____

This Page Not Used.

PROBLEM 15-3 ___

1. and 2.

JOURNAL

	DATE	DESCRIPTION	POST. REF.	DEBIT	CREDIT	
1						1
2						2
3						3
4						4
5						5
6						6
7						7
8						8
9						9
10						10
11						11
12						12
13						13
14						14
15						15
16						16
17						17
18						18
19						19
20						20
21						21
22						22
23						23
24						24
25						25

3.

_____

_____

4.

_____

_____

_____

_____

592

This Page Not Used.

PROBLEM 15-4 ___

1.

JOURNAL   PAGE _____

	DATE	DESCRIPTION	POST. REF.	DEBIT	CREDIT	
1						1
2						2
3						3
4						4
5						5
6						6
7						7
8						8
9						9
10						10
11						11
12						12
13						13
14						14
15						15
16						16
17						17
18						18
19						19
20						20
21						21
22						22
23						23
24						24
25						25
26						26
27						27
28						28
29						29
30						30
31						31
32						32
33						33
34						34
35						35
36						36

PROBLEM 15-4 ___, Concluded

2. (a) 2007: _____

   (b) 2008: _____

3.

PROBLEM 15-5 ___

JOURNAL

PAGE ____

	DATE	DESCRIPTION	POST. REF.	DEBIT	CREDIT	
1						1
2						2
3						3
4						4
5						5
6						6
7						7
8						8
9						9
10						10
11						11
12						12
13						13
14						14
15						15
16						16
17						17
18						18
19						19
20						20
21						21
22						22
23						23
24						24
25						25
26						26
27						27
28						28
29						29
30						30
31						31
32						32
33						33
34						34
35						35
36						36

This Page Not Used.

APPENDIX PROBLEM 15-6 ___

1. a. and b.

JOURNAL

PAGE

	DATE		DESCRIPTION	POST. REF.	DEBIT	CREDIT	
1							1
2							2
3							3
4							4
5							5
6							6
7							7
8							8
9							9
10							10
11							11
12							12
13							13
14							14
15							15
16							16
17							17
18							18
19							19

2.

_____

_____

_____

This Page Not Used.

APPENDIX PROBLEM 15-7 ___

1. a. and b.

	DATE	DESCRIPTION	POST. REF.	DEBIT	CREDIT	
1						1
2						2
3						3
4						4
5						5
6						6
7						7
8						8
9						9
10						10
11						11
12						12
13						13
14						14
15						15
16						16
17						17
18						18
19						19

JOURNAL   PAGE

2.

_____

_____

_____

_____

_____

_____

This Page Not Used.

COMPREHENSIVE PROBLEM 4

1.

JOURNAL   PAGE

	DATE		DESCRIPTION	POST. REF.	DEBIT	CREDIT	
1							1
2							2
3							3
4							4
5							5
6							6
7							7
8							8
9							9
10							10
11							11
12							12
13							13
14							14
15							15
16							16
17							17
18							18
19							19
20							20
21							21
22							22
23							23
24							24
25							25
26							26
27							27
28							28
29							29
30							30
31							31
32							32
33							33
34							34
35							35
36							36

COMPREHENSIVE PROBLEM 4, Continued

JOURNAL   PAGE

	DATE		DESCRIPTION	POST. REF.	DEBIT	CREDIT	
1							1
2							2
3							3
4							4
5							5
6							6
7							7
8							8
9							9
10							10
11							11
12							12
13							13
14							14
15							15
16							16
17							17
18							18
19							19
20							20
21							21
22							22
23							23
24							24
25							25
26							26
27							27
28							28
29							29
30							30
31							31
32							32
33							33
34							34
35							35
36							36

COMPREHENSIVE PROBLEM 4, Continued

JOURNAL

PAGE

	DATE	DESCRIPTION	POST. REF.	DEBIT	CREDIT	
1						1
2						2
3						3
4						4
5						5
6						6
7						7
8						8
9						9
10						10
11						11
12						12
13						13
14						14
15						15
16						16
17						17
18						18
19						19
20						20
21						21
22						22
23						23
24						24
25						25
26						26
27						27
28						28
29						29
30						30
31						31
32						32
33						33
34						34
35						35
36						36

COMPREHENSIVE PROBLEM 4, Continued

2. a. *Omit "00" in the cents columns.*

Income Statement

COMPREHENSIVE PROBLEM 4, Continued

Income Statement (Concluded)						

COMPREHENSIVE PROBLEM 4, Continued

2. b. *Omit "00" in the cents columns.*

Retained Earnings Statement

COMPREHENSIVE PROBLEM 4, Continued

2. c. *Omit "00" in the cents columns.*

Balance Sheet

COMPREHENSIVE PROBLEM 4, Concluded

	Balance Sheet (Concluded)								

EXERCISE 16-1

_____

_____

_____

_____

_____

_____

_____

_____

_____

_____

_____

_____

_____

EXERCISE 16-2

a. _____

b. _____

c. _____

d. _____

e. _____

f. _____

g. _____

h. _____

EXERCISE 16-3

a. Issued preferred stock: _____

b. Net income: _____

c. Sold equipment: _____

d. Purchased treasury stock: _____

e. Purchases buildings: _____

f. Purchased patents: _____

g. Issued bonds: _____

h. Issued common stock: _____

i. Sold long-term investments: _____

j. Paid cash dividends: _____

k. Redeemed bonds: _____

EXERCISE 16-4

a. Gain on retirement of long-term debt: _____

b. Increase in merchandise inventory: _____

c. Amortization of patent: _____

d. Decrease in accounts receivable: _____

e. Depreciation of fixed assets: _____

f. Decrease in prepaid expenses: _____

g. Decrease in salaries payable: _____

h. Increase in notes receivable due in 90 days from customers: _____

i. Decrease in accounts payable: _____

j. Loss on disposal of fixed assets: _____

k. Increase in notes payable due in 90 days to vendors: _____

EXERCISE 16-5

EXERCISE 16-6

a.

b. _____

_____

_____

EXERCISE 16-7

EXERCISE 16-8

EXERCISE 16-9

EXERCISE 16-10

EXERCISE 16-11

EXERCISE 16-12

EXERCISE 16-13

EXERCISE 16-14

EXERCISE 16-15

EXERCISE 16-16

a.

b.

EXERCISE 16-17

EXERCISE 16-18

EXERCISE 16-19

a. and b.

EXERCISE 16-20

EXERCISE 16-21

a.

b.

EXERCISE 16-22

EXERCISE 16-23

EXERCISE 16-24

EXERCISE 16-25

	FISCAL YEAR ENDED JANUARY 29, 2006				

PROBLEM 16-1 ___

PROBLEM 16-1 ___ , Concluded

The use of this form is not required unless so indicated by the instructor.

	A	B	C	D	E	F	G	
	End-of-Period Spreadsheet (Work Sheet) for Statement of Cash Flows							
	Accounts	**Balance** _____, 20__		**Transactions** Dr.	Cr.	**Balance** _____,20__		
1								1
2								2
3								3
4								4
5								5
6								6
7								7
8								8
9								9
10								10
11								11
12								12
13								13
14								14
15								15
16								16
17								17
18								18
19								19
20								20
21								21
22								22
23								23
24								24
25								25
26								26
27								27
28								28
29								29
30								30
31								31
32								32
33								33
34								34
35								35
36								36
37								37
38								38
39								39
40								40

PROBLEM 16-2 ___

Omit "00" in the cents columns.

PROBLEM 16-2 ___ , Continued

The use of this form is not required unless so indicated by the instructor.

	A	B	C	D	E	F	G	
	End-of-Period Spreadsheet (Work Sheet) for Statement of Cash Flows							
	Accounts	**Balance**		**Transactions**		**Balance**		
		_____, 20__		**Dr.**	**Cr.**	**_____,20__**		
1								1
2								2
3								3
4								4
5								5
6								6
7								7
8								8
9								9
10								10
11								11
12								12
13								13
14								14
15								15
16								16
17								17
18								18
19								19
20								20
21								21
22								22
23								23
24								24
25								25
26								26
27								27
28								28
29								29
30								30
31								31
32								32
33								33
34								34
35								35
36								36
37								37
38								38
39								39
40								40

PROBLEM 16-3 ___

Omit "00" in the cents columns.

PROBLEM 16-3 ___, Continued

PROBLEM 16-3 ____, Concluded

End-of-Period Spreadsheet (Work Sheet) for Statement of Cash Flows

	Accounts	Balance _____, 20__		Transactions Dr.	Cr.	Balance _____,20__		
1								1
2								2
3								3
4								4
5								5
6								6
7								7
8								8
9								9
10								10
11								11
12								12
13								13
14								14
15								15
16								16
17								17
18								18
19								19
20								20
21								21
22								22
23								23
24								24
25								25
26								26
27								27
28								28
29								29
30								30
31								31
32								32
33								33
34								34
35								35
36								36
37								37
38								38
39								39
40								40

630

This Page Not Used.

PROBLEM 16-4 ___

Omit "00" in the cents columns.

PROBLEM 16-4 ___ , Concluded

Computations

PROBLEM 16-5 ___

Omit "00" in the cents columns.

PROBLEM 16-5 ___ , Concluded

Computations

EXERCISE 17-1

a.

_____
_____

	2008		2007	
	AMOUNT	PERCENT	AMOUNT	PERCENT

b. _____
_____
_____
_____
_____
_____
_____
_____
_____
_____
_____
_____
_____
_____
_____

EXERCISE 17-2

a.

_____

_____

_____

	FISCAL YEAR 2004		FISCAL YEAR 2003	
	AMOUNT	PERCENT	AMOUNT	PERCENT

b. _____

_____

_____

_____

_____

_____

_____

_____

_____

_____

_____

_____

_____

_____

_____

_____

_____

EXERCISE 17-3

a.

_____
_____
_____

	JARIBO COMMUNICATIONS COMPANY		COMMUNI-CATIONS INDUSTRY AVERAGE
	AMOUNT	PERCENT	PERCENT

b. _____
_____
_____
_____
_____
_____
_____
_____
_____
_____
_____
_____

EXERCISE 17-4

	2008		2007	
	AMOUNT	PERCENT	AMOUNT	PERCENT

EXERCISE 17-5

a. _____

	2008	2007	INCREASE (DECREASE)	
	AMOUNT	AMOUNT	AMOUNT	PERCENT

b. _____

EXERCISE 17-6

a. (1) _____

_____

_____

_____

_____

_____

_____

(2) _____

_____

_____

_____

_____

_____

(3) _____

_____

_____

_____

_____

_____

b. _____

_____

_____

_____

_____

_____

_____

_____

_____

_____

_____

EXERCISE 17-7

a. (1) _____

_____

(2) _____

b. _____

EXERCISE 17-8

a. _____

b. _____

EXERCISE 17-9

a. (1) _____

_____

_____

_____

_____

_____

_____

_____

(2) _____

_____

_____

_____

_____

_____

_____

_____

b. _____

_____

_____

_____

_____

_____

_____

_____

_____

_____

_____

_____

_____

_____

_____

EXERCISE 17-10

a. (1) _____

_____

_____

_____

_____

_____

_____

_____

(2) _____

_____

_____

_____

_____

_____

_____

_____

_____

b. _____

_____

_____

_____

_____

_____

_____

_____

_____

_____

_____

_____

_____

_____

EXERCISE 17-11

a. (1) _____

_____

_____

_____

_____

_____

_____

_____

(2) _____

_____

_____

_____

_____

_____

_____

_____

_____

_____

b. _____

_____

_____

_____

_____

_____

_____

_____

_____

_____

_____

_____

_____

_____

_____

EXERCISE 17-12

a. (1) _____

_____

_____

_____

_____

_____

_____

_____

_____

_____

(2) _____

_____

_____

_____

_____

_____

_____

_____

_____

_____

b. _____

_____

_____

_____

_____

_____

_____

_____

_____

_____

_____

_____

_____

_____

EXERCISE 17-13

a. _____

b. _____

c. _____

EXERCISE 17-14

a. _____

b. _____

c. _____

EXERCISE 17-15

a. _____

b. _____

c. _____

EXERCISE 17-16

a. _____

EXERCISE 17-17

a. _____
_____
_____
_____
_____
_____
_____
_____
_____
_____
_____
_____
_____
_____
_____
_____
_____
_____
_____
_____
_____
_____

b. _____
_____
_____
_____
_____
_____
_____
_____
_____
_____
_____
_____
_____

EXERCISE 17-18

a. _____

b. _____

c. _____

d. _____

EXERCISE 17-19

a. _____

b. _____

c. _____

d. _____

e. _____

f. _____

EXERCISE 17-20

a. _____

b. _____

c. _____

d. _____

e. _____

f. _____

EXERCISE 17-21

a. _____

b. _____

c. _____

d. _____

EXERCISE 17-22

a. _____

b. _____

EXERCISE 17-23

a. _____

b. _____

PROBLEM 17-1 ___

1.

	2008	2007	INCREASE (DECREASE)	
			AMOUNT	PERCENT

Comparative Income Statement

PROBLEM 17-1 ___ , Concluded

2.

PROBLEM 17-2 ___

1.

	Comparative Income Statement				
	2008			2007	
	AMOUNT	PERCENT		AMOUNT	PERCENT

PROBLEM 17-2 ____, Concluded

2.

PROBLEM 17-3 ___

1. a. _____

_____

_____

_____

_____

_____

_____

_____

_____

b. _____

_____

_____

_____

_____

_____

_____

_____

_____

_____

c. _____

_____

_____

_____

_____

_____

_____

_____

_____

_____

_____

PROBLEM 17-3 ___, Concluded

2.

Transaction	Working Capital	Current Ratio	Quick Ratio
a.			
b.			
c.			
d.			
e.			
f.			
g.			
h.			
i.			
j.			

Supporting calculations:

_____

_____

_____

_____

_____

_____

_____

_____

_____

_____

_____

_____

_____

_____

_____

_____

_____

PROBLEM 17-4 ___

1. through 19.

1. _____

Ratio	Numerator	Denominator	Calculated Value
2.			
3.			
4.			
5.			
6.			
7.			
8.			
9.			
10.			
11.			
12.			
13.			
14.			
15.			
16.			

PROBLEM 17-4 ___, Concluded

Ratio	Numerator	Denominator	Calculated Value
17.			
18.			
19.			

PROBLEM 17-5 ___

1. a.

Rate earned on total assets

Year

Computations _____
_____
_____
_____
_____
_____

PROBLEM 17-5 ___, Continued

1. b.

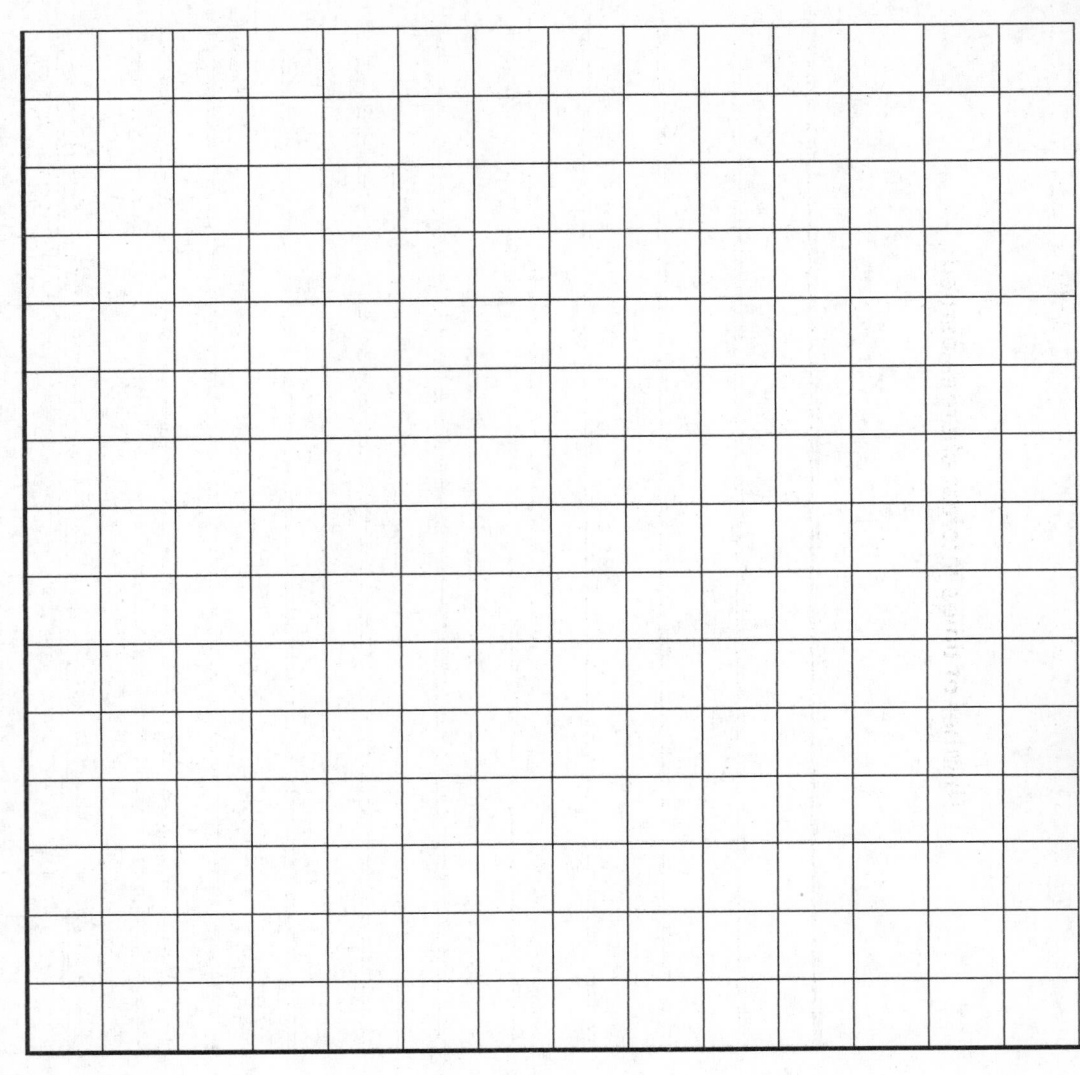

Rate earned on stockholders' equity

Year

Computations _____

_____

_____

_____

_____

_____

PROBLEM 17-5 ___, Continued

1. c.

Number of times interest charges earned

Year

Computations _____

_____

_____

_____

_____

_____

_____

PROBLEM 17-5 ___, Continued

1. d.

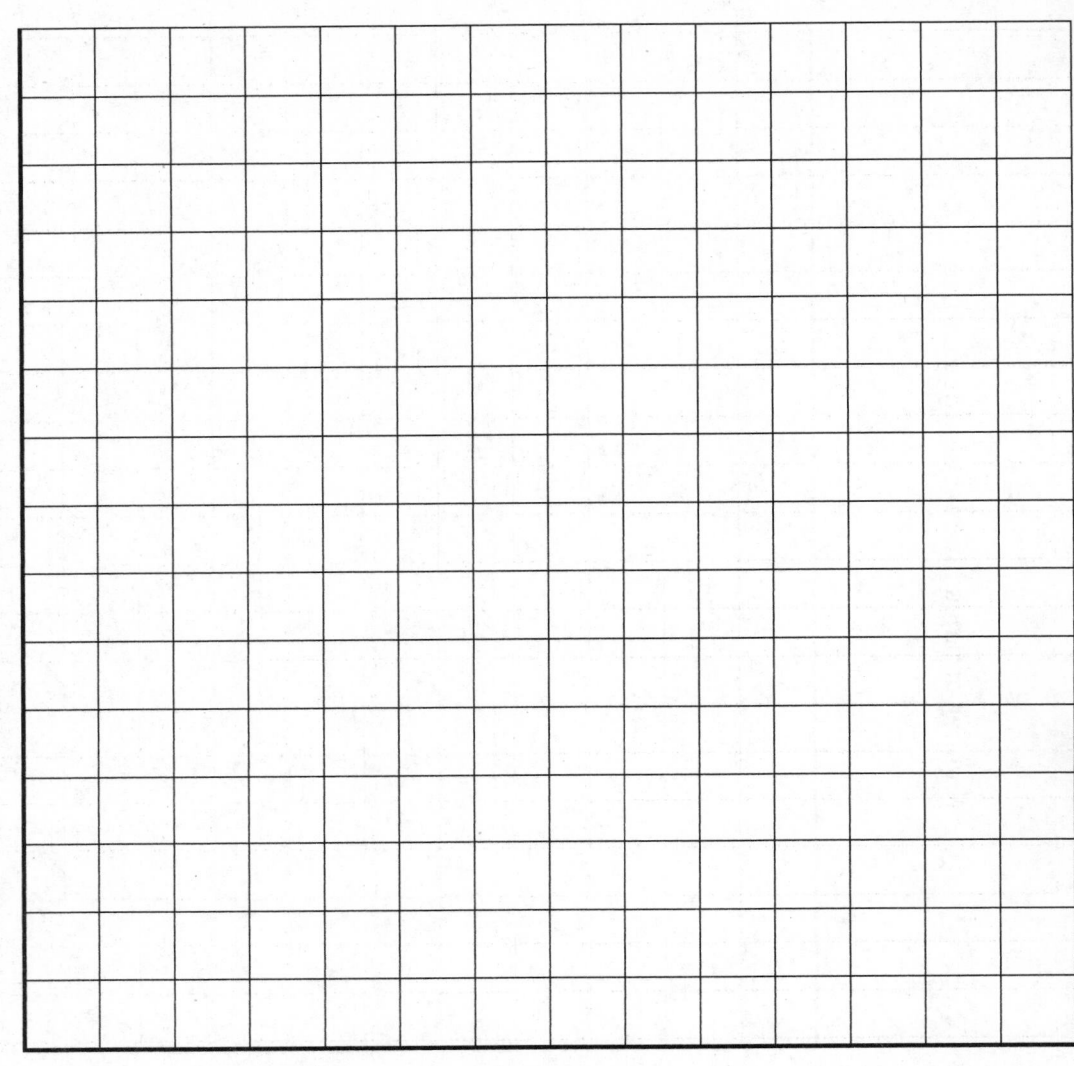

Ratio of liabilities to stockholders' equity

Year

Computations

PROBLEM 17-5 ___ , Concluded

2.

This Page Not Used.

WILLIAMS-SONOMA, PROBLEM

1. a. through m.

_____

_____

_____

_____

_____

_____

_____

_____

_____

_____

_____

_____

_____

_____

_____

_____

_____

_____

_____

_____

_____

_____

_____

_____

_____

_____

_____

_____

_____

_____

_____

WILLIAMS-SONOMA, PROBLEM, Continued

WILLIAMS-SONOMA, PROBLEM, Continued

2. a. through m.

_____

WILLIAMS-SONOMA, PROBLEM, Concluded

EXERCISE B-1

a.–b.

JOURNAL   PAGE

	DATE		DESCRIPTION	POST. REF.	DEBIT	CREDIT	
1							1
2							2
3							3
4							4
5							5
6							6
7							7
8							8
9							9
10							10
11							11
12							12
13							13

EXERCISE B-2

a.–b.

JOURNAL   PAGE

	DATE		DESCRIPTION	POST. REF.	DEBIT	CREDIT	
1							1
2							2
3							3
4							4
5							5
6							6
7							7
8							8
9							9
10							10
11							11
12							12
13							13

EXERCISE B-3

a. (1) _____

  (2) _____

  (3) _____

  (4) _____

  (5) _____

b. (1)–(5)

JOURNAL   PAGE

	DATE	DESCRIPTION	POST. REF.	DEBIT	CREDIT	
1						1
2						2
3						3
4						4
5						5
6						6
7						7
8						8
9						9
10						10
11						11
12						12
13						13
14						14
15						15
16						16
17						17
18						18
19						19
20						20

EXERCISE   B-4

a. (1) _____

   (2) _____

   (3) _____

   (4) _____

   (5) _____

b. (1)–(5)

JOURNAL

PAGE

	DATE	DESCRIPTION	POST. REF.	DEBIT	CREDIT	
1						1
2						2
3						3
4						4
5						5
6						6
7						7
8						8
9						9
10						10
11						11
12						12
13						13
14						14
15						15
16						16
17						17
18						18
19						19
20						20

This Page Not Used.

PROBLEM C-1

1.

End-of-Period Spreadsheet (Work Sheet)

	Unadjusted Trial Balance		Adjustments		Adjusted Trial Balance		Income Statement		Balance Sheet	
Account Title	Dr.	Cr.	Dr.	Cr.	Dr.	Cr.	Dr.	Cr.	Dr.	Cr.
1										
2										
3										
4										
5										
6										
7										
8										
9										
10										
11										
12										
13										
14										
15										
16										
17										
18										
19										
20										
21										
22										
23										
24										
25										

Name _____

PROBLEM C-1, Continued

Appendix C

End-of-Period Spreadsheet (Work Sheet)
—Continued

	Account Title	Unadjusted Trial Balance Dr.	Unadjusted Trial Balance Cr.	Adjustments Dr.	Adjustments Cr.	Adjusted Trial Balance Dr.	Adjusted Trial Balance Cr.	Income Statement Dr.	Income Statement Cr.	Balance Sheet Dr.	Balance Sheet Cr.	
26												26
27												27
28												28
29												29
30												30
31												31
32												32
33												33
34												34
35												35
36												36
37												37
38												38
39												39
40												40
41												41
42												42
43												43
44												44
45												45
46												46
47												47
48												48
49												49
50												50

PROBLEM C-1, Continued

2.

Income Statement

PROBLEM C-1, Continued

3.

Statement of Owner's Equity				

Name _____

PROBLEM C-1, Continued

4.

Balance Sheet

PROBLEM C-1

5. <div align="center">**JOURNAL**</div> PAGE 3

	DATE		DESCRIPTION	POST. REF.	DEBIT	CREDIT	
1			*Adjusting Entries*				1
2							2
3							3
4							4
5							5
6							6
7							7
8							8
9							9
10							10
11							11
12							12
13							13
14							14
15							15
16							16
17							17
18							18
19							19
20							20
21							21
22							22
23							23
24							24
25							25
26							26
27							27
28							28
29							29
30							30
31							31
32							32
33							33
34							34
35							35

PROBLEM C-1, Concluded

6.   **JOURNAL**   PAGE 3

	DATE		DESCRIPTION	POST. REF.	DEBIT	CREDIT	
1			*Closing Entries*				1
2							2
3							3
4							4
5							5
6							6
7							7
8							8
9							9
10							10
11							11
12							12
13							13
14							14
15							15
16							16
17							17
18							18
19							19
20							20
21							21
22							22
23							23
24							24
25							25
26							26
27							27
28							28
29							29
30							30

This Page Not Used.

PROBLEM C-2

1.

		End-of-Period Spreadsheet (Work Sheet)								
	A	B	C	D	E	F	G	H	I	J	K
Account Title		Unadjusted Trial Balance		Adjustments		Adjusted Trial Balance		Income Statement		Balance Sheet	
		Dr.	Cr.	Dr.	Cr.	Dr.	Cr.	Dr.	Cr.	Dr.	Cr.
1											
2											
3											
4											
5											
6											
7											
8											
9											
10											
11											
12											
13											
14											
15											
16											
17											
18											
19											
20											
21											
22											
23											
24											
25											

Name _____

PROBLEM C-2, Continued

Appendix C

End-of-Period Spreadsheet (Work Sheet)—Continued

Account Title	Unadjusted Trial Balance Dr.	Unadjusted Trial Balance Cr.	Adjustments Dr.	Adjustments Cr.	Adjusted Trial Balance Dr.	Adjusted Trial Balance Cr.	Income Statement Dr.	Income Statement Cr.	Balance Sheet Dr.	Balance Sheet Cr.	
											26
											27
											28
											29
											30
											31
											32
											33
											34
											35
											36
											37
											38
											39
											40
											41
											42
											43
											44
											45
											46
											47
											48
											49
											50

PROBLEM C-2, Continued

2.

	Income Statement						

PROBLEM C-2, Continued

3.

Statement of Owner's Equity							

Name _____

PROBLEM C-2, Continued

4.

Balance Sheet

PROBLEM C-2

5.

JOURNAL

PAGE 3

	DATE		DESCRIPTION	POST. REF.	DEBIT	CREDIT	
1			*Adjusting Entries*				1
2							2
3							3
4							4
5							5
6							6
7							7
8							8
9							9
10							10
11							11
12							12
13							13
14							14
15							15
16							16
17							17
18							18
19							19
20							20
21							21
22							22
23							23
24							24
25							25
26							26
27							27
28							28
29							29
30							30
31							31
32							32
33							33
34							34
35							35

PROBLEM C-2, Concluded

6.

				JOURNAL																PAGE 3			

	DATE		DESCRIPTION	POST. REF.	DEBIT	CREDIT	
1			*Closing Entries*				1
2							2
3							3
4							4
5							5
6							6
7							7
8							8
9							9
10							10
11							11
12							12
13							13
14							14
15							15
16							16
17							17
18							18
19							19
20							20
21							21
22							22
23							23
24							24
25							25
26							26
27							27
28							28
29							29
30							30